Make My Brand Bigger

"My formal education and early career endeavors solidly embraced finance and economics as the primary disciplines that contributed to the success of businesses and professional enterprises. I'm also the founder of five successful startup businesses.

At an early age, my beliefs constructed my views of subjects like marketing and branding as being too esoteric and difficult to quantify. I was wrong.

Within the pages of this book, Alex Valderrama has clearly portrayed the essential path(s) to creating and sustaining a successful business by beginning with the branding process.

His brand building process, which is explicitly described in this book, demonstrates that taking the precise and often complex steps through the branding experience will significantly improve the prospect of business success.

Alex has eliminated any notion of "esoteric" within the branding and marketing process. He has merged the essential tools of art and science to articulate the importance of traveling through the branding experience with a highly detailed strategy.

Perhaps the most enlightening aspect of this book depicts the importance of collaborating throughout the branding building process with a seasoned professional who can skillfully augment this oftentimes complicated process."
Jeff Bernard, MBA

Alex Valderrama knows how a brand is built and he takes great pains to point out that the old saw of making a logo bigger on a print ad or a billboard is not the same as building a brand.

"Make My Brand Bigger" is a tremendous primer for anyone working in any industry where a brand name is important. Alex hashes out the silly pre- and mis-conceptions and establishes that building a brand is an ongoing project, one that never ends and one that can never get boring.

Highly recommended reading!

Scott Forbes

Make My Brand Bigger

Copyright © 2018 by Alexander S. Valderrama

All rights reserved. No part of this publication may be reproduced, distributed, or transmitted in any form or by any means, including photocopying, recording, or other electronic or mechanical methods, without the prior written permission of the publisher, except in the case of brief quotations embodied in critical reviews and certain other noncommercial uses permitted by copyright law.

ISBN: 9781730704239 (Paper Back)

This book was inspired by true events.

Book design and front cover image
by Cranium Agency LLC

www.craniumagency.com

2nd Edition 2018.

Make My Brand Bigger

LEARN HOW TO
UNCOVER YOUR BRAND'S SECRET SAUCE

PLUS, BUILD A STRONG
AND SUSTAINABLE BRAND

By Alexander S. Valderrama

2ND EDITION 2018

Make My Brand Bigger

Acknowledgments

I once heard a story about Picasso. A woman walking along a beach notices a person sitting comfortably on a beach chair and asks, "Hey, are you Picasso?" The older gentleman replies, "Yes I am, why do you ask?" The woman, excited beyond belief, asks Picasso, "Oh my, can you draw a picture of me?" Picasso, being a polite gentleman, responds, "Sure, let me get my drawing book and pencil." Picasso proceeds to draw the woman and spends about five minutes. He then tears the drawing out of his sketchbook and gives it to her. Excited, she says, "This is amazing, can I give you $20 for it?" With a slight frown Picasso says "No, that will be $500." Her hand on her hips, the woman asks, "How can you possibly ask for $500 when it only took you five minutes to draw?" Picasso takes a second to compose himself and says, "Actually, ma'am, this has taken me 40 years to perfect."

This story rings true for everyone who has a passion for what they do. I, like you, have devoted many years to my craft. My livelihood depends on my ability to execute a service which is beyond my competitors' service and also fills the needs of my clients. I sense the same passion from the leadership of my clients.

Thanks to all my clients who afforded me the opportunity to fine-tune my craft of brand building. I've had the pleasure of working with clients such as Microsoft, Wells Fargo, Massey Ferguson, Maytag, IBM, and many more.

Thanks to my great team of friends, Wendy Terrien, Jeff Bernard, David Avrin, Dave Schachter, Andy Kamlet, Scott Forbes, and Leanne Johnson who provided sound advice and helped me get this book off the ground.

A special thanks to my wife Laurie and my two children, Nathan and Sarah, for the support and allowing me the freedom to work endless hours building my business and writing this book.

Also, over time, I have developed a deep admiration for my closest friends and truly appreciate the support they have provided.

Finally, I have come across some exceptional and smart people in my life. I am grateful to have met these people and appreciate the opportunity to learn from them.

Make My Brand Bigger

Contents

Author's Note: Why should I make my brand bigger?   10

Chapter 1: Your Brand's Secret Sauce   13

Chapter 2: Discovery and Gap Analysis   19
- 2.1 Company Details
- 2.2 Legal Assistance for Brand Clearance, Ownership, and Protection
- 2.3 Brand Elements
- 2.4 Marketing and Sales
- 2.5 Visual Brand Audit
- 2.6 Wrap Up

Chapter 3: What's in a Name   51

Chapter 4: Brand Building   59
- 4.1 Brand Purpose
- 4.2 Brand Character and Personality
- 4.3 The Tone
- 4.4 Brand Essence
- 4.5 Brand Values
- 4.6 Differentiators
- 4.7 Let's Talk About POSITIONING
- 4.8 Value Proposition and Brand Story

Chapter 5: Customer Experience   92

Chapter 6: Marketing and Sales   100
- 6.1 Your Customer
- 6.2 Competitors
- 6.3 Market Analysis

    6.4 Market Size
    6.5 Market Segments
    6.6 Channels and Distribution
    6.7 Budget
    6.8 Marketing Tactics
    6.9 Wrap Up

Chapter 7: Visual Communications   126
    7.1 Logos and Colors
    7.2 Brand Identity
    7.3 Brand Standards
    7.4 Wrap Up

Chapter 8: Pre-Launch and Launch Planning   137
    8.1 Let's Get Organized
    8.2 Pre-Launch Implementation
    8.3 Launch Implementation: Internal
    8.4 Launch Implementation: External
    8.5 Wrap Up

Chapter 9: Post-Launch, Analysis, and Refinement   151
    9.1 Post-Launch Goals and Objectives
    9.2 Post-Launch Marketing and Sales
    9.3 Brand Champions
    9.4 Review Brand Message and Story

Final Thoughts   156

Brand Terminology   157

About the Author   162

Author's Note

Make My Brand Bigger is meant to provide you with a concise summary of decades of branding experience. Many strategies depicted are what some people in the branding industry consider "trade secrets." In the past years, as I work solving branding issues with many clients, the typical question arose, "Why don't you write a book on branding?" Well, I have to admit; my biggest contemplation was providing too much information and giving away what has taken me decades to understand and learn. After a thorough contemplation, I decided to lay out a rough draft of my book and share it with several of my close friends and clients. The initial feedback was very positive, so I then decided to illustrate the brand building process and share it with everyone.

I truly hope you will find the information enclosed helpful, to the point it will make an impact on your business, profession and life.

Each chapter is devoted to a particular topic of brand building. My experiences and expertise are derived from working alongside many smart people.

Depending on your unique situation, you may need to dig a little deeper to gain a better understanding of each topic in the book. You might find it helpful to read the whole book prior to tackling each exercise. This will give you an overall comprehensive grasp of the different strategies, tactics, phases, steps, etc.

So, who should read a book about brand building?

Make My Brand Bigger was written for entrepreneurs, sole proprietors, marketers, product managers, students, and anyone in charge of a rebrand initiative or the launch of a new brand. And of course, anyone who wants to have major success building a brand.

This book is meant to help take you through the journey of building a brand from concept to launch and post-launch. It will also be an excellent resource for the further development of an existing brand. During a rebrand, we will use the initial gap analysis to uncover significant disconnects between where the brand currently stands and where we want to be. You will be able to use the information discovered in the gap analysis and apply it to a road map of brand building elements noted in the subsequent chapters, that need to be added, fixed or altered to fit your brand vision.

On a side note, I truly believe great brands are born from the passion of a person's attempt to impact other's lives. This passion should transcend through the brand internally and externally.

Finally, do you have an existing brand and want to learn how to move it forward, create better brand loyalty, increase brand equity, and win more business? *Make My Brand Bigger* will help you uncover areas where you can improve your brand's "Secret Sauce," and show you how to tackle specific brand issues with new ideas.

CHAPTER ONE

Your Brand's Secret Sauce

You may wonder why I renamed my book from "Make My Logo Bigger" to *"Make My Brand Bigger."*

Well, based on my experience, many entrepreneurs and people in charge of making major decisions about the direction of a brand have false impressions about how to execute a successful brand awareness and strategy. They have an instinctive, although misguided, solution to enlarge their logo and make it as big as possible on communication materials. Hence, I can tell you too many times I have heard a new client suggest the best solution to branding effectiveness is to "make my logo bigger." Most of the time the problem is not the visibility and size of their logo,

Make My Brand Bigger

it is an overall strategic issue of their brand message and effectiveness. *When a client simply wants to make their logo bigger, it is a reaction to a more significant issue of a struggling brand.* Typically, this reaction is not a visceral one, but a lack of understanding of what should have been done earlier in the brand development.

Make My Brand Bigger became a meme for the idea of exploring ways to make a brand more visible and create a meaningful, intuitive, and emotional connection between the brand and the customer. *Make My Brand Bigger* is a metaphor for creating a brand that not only gets noticed but also makes an impact on peoples' lives. It is all about launching a new brand through the lens of creating a strong connection with your customers.

Recently, we had the great opportunity to work with a new client that owns and operates a car wash. The client has been in business for over 25 years and as part of our discovery process we inquired into what makes them different and separates them from their competitors. After several sessions we were surprised to learn how complicated the detail car wash business is. There are a lot of areas that need to be precisely accurate in their day-to-day operations. Take for example the need to comply with city, state, and federal regulations. The ongoing task of educating their employees on new techniques, processes, and equipment usage. The ongoing evaluation of new and safer chemicals which are used to clean the exterior and interior of a car. All of these needs are complex and difficult to execute, and they are quite complex. My point is that most companies spend a significant amount of time creating their "Secret Sauce" primarily in the development of their product or service. The development of a product or service can take several months to many years, not to mention the enormous amount of money needed to bring it to market.

However, discovering and defining your brand's "Secret Sauce", that is used hundreds, thousands, and in some cases millions of times in all marketing and sales communications to acquire and retain new customers, are often overlooked or are considered a low business priority. The importance of creating and defining your brand's "Secret Sauce" are equally as critical to the success of your business.

So, why is it so important to clearly define your brand's "Secret Sauce"?

Let me begin by interjecting the idea that not all brands are created equal. As previously mentioned, many companies do not devote the time necessary to develop a thorough understanding of their brand which results in missing many critical communication opportunities and saves the company from wasted efforts with misdirected advertisements and campaigns. Too often when we work with new clients, the outcome of the initial brand gap analysis raises many questions about their current state of brand strategy and their engagement with various marketing channels such as magazine advertising, social media engagement, and trade show participation. After careful research, some of these tactics are often identified as an enormous amount of wasted time and money.

Great brands are successful not only by defining a unique offering to their customers, but also by creating a unique position in the marketplace. This is accomplished by working through various elements of your brand such as brand positioning, messaging, differentiators, competitive position, brand story, SWOT analysis, brand character, tone, and more. It may sound like a lot of branding jargon that means very little on the surface, but all of these brand elements—and more—help to define your brand's "Secret Sauce." In essence, a well-articulated brand will separate your brand from your competitors, assist in creating your overall brand message, define your unique story, and motivate your customers to act.

Your Brand's Secret Sauce

A brand must take on a holistic approach and encompass every single aspect of the company, including the brand name, leadership of the principals, the culture, the product offerings, the service offerings, high-level benefits, the location of the business, company values, community involvement, associations, etc. You get the point.

Furthermore, developing a robust brand strategy is paramount to the success of your business. This strategy can also make a significant difference in your team's ability to successfully launch a strong marketing and sales strategy. We regularly talk to marketing and sales teams. One of their biggest complaints is the lack of a unique brand message or story that helps them define a preference for their prospects.

Once you have developed a strong brand strategy, your very own brand "Secret Sauce," you will be able to articulate and define your unique brand story and motivate your potential customer to act. And finally, your marketing and sales teams will be able to use your brand's "Secret Sauce" to develop a sound marketing and sales strategy.

Moreover, getting people motivated to purchase your product or service starts with a strong brand story.

There are many nuances to brand building. Over the past three decades, my experience working with incredible branding experts has brought me to share some great insights, divulge intellectual knowledge, and provide specific agency processes. *Make My Brand Bigger* will help you alleviate costly mistakes and uncover specific details on how to rebrand or build your next brand.

I often hear, "You work with big brands that can afford to develop brand strategies, it's just too expensive for us." Remember, big brands technically reach a lot more people. If you are working on a smaller brand the cost should be scaled accordingly. Plus, big brand haven't cornered the market on great branding. All the ideas and strategies depicted in this book can be applied to a national brand or a small, locally-based brand.

I have a lot of information for you. As we go through this journey of brand building, we will touch on many strategies and delve deep into others.

So, let's get started...

CHAPTER TWO

Discovery and Gap Analysis

In this chapter of discovery and gap analysis, we will review the critical elements to help you rebrand and reposition an existing brand or build a new brand. The discovery and gap phase is the first step in uncovering the status of your brand along with its critical elements. We will use this phase to build a strong foundation and successfully launch your brand. We will also use this phase to outline key components that should be considered in your discovery process.

Every business is unique. A templated branding approach will not always apply to every company. Every time I work with a new client, I find myself modifying aspects of the brand building process. It is important to note each business situation is very unique and each brand has distinctive qualities.

Several months ago, we were hired to work with a telecommunications company that primarily focuses on rural markets. The company had been in business for a long time and struggled to grow their monthly subscriptions.

Through our discovery and gap analysis, our first task was to discover their current state of business and gather a list of brand message gaps. One advantage of working with an existing company is utilizing our ability to glean the results and failures from information associated with the company's previous marketing strategy. After several months of research, we were able to identify key brand elements that were missing in their brand story. One of the most important elements they had not defined in their previous brand explorations was their brand essence. Due to the lack of a clear and definitive brand essence, they had struggled to convey a critical aspect of their brand story. Eventually, our brand research brought us to uncover their brand essence as being "neighborly." This might seem simple, although by design it was a clear indication of who they were at the core of their brand. We will talk more about the brand essence in Chapter 4.

Discovery and Gap Analysis

Ultimately, with the refinement of their brand message, brand story, and articulation of their unique position in the market, their sales and revenue increased.

You may have heard the phrase, "Knowledge is Power." To me this means, "The more you know about a particular subject, the more you are prepared to make good decisions." Understanding your brand with high detail will help guide your decisions in a clear and focused way.

The phase of discovery and gap analysis is by far one of the most exhaustive. Once you have discovered and thoroughly analyzed your gaps, you will have a strong foundation for the other sections.

The areas listed below are intended to provide you with a framework for evaluating and understanding your brand.

- Company Details
- Legal Needs
- Brand Elements
- Marketing and Sales
- Also, The Wrap Up: Key tips you should think about when you go through the discovery process.

The goal is to discover, document and compile all the information you have on your brand, what needs further research, and what needs to be created.

The discovery and gap analysis is the process of understanding the gaps in your brand and also closing those gaps to create a well-organized summary.

2.1 Company Details

Uncovering the gaps in your company structure is key to developing your brand. Therefore, closing these gaps are essential to the success of your brand.

This is the first step to understanding your business contextually. The exercise is designed to help you gather the main details of your business and also uncover where you might need to develop additional information to help build your brand.

(1) Business Objectives

While a business plan is important to the success of a company, your business objectives will help you plan for the future. These objectives will most likely evolve based on internal and external factors such as product availability, the economy, trends, new competitors, etc. Setting your business objectives provides a coherent plan that you can share with your team and allows them to understand your direction. This is a great time to define or refine your business objectives to help you grow.

Discovery and Gap Analysis

To get started make a list of your business goals, short-term and long-term, and begin to develop these goals if you don't already have them. The basic intent is to begin setting your business goals. These goals will then be turned into an overall strategic plan that can be tactfully executed. Below are several questions to consider.

- Are there areas of your business that need improvement?
- What market share do you aspire to have in a given time frame?
- How will you determine if you are successful or not. What are the metrics?
- What is the vision for your company in 1, 2, 5-year increments?
- What are your 1, 2, 5-year revenue projections?
- How do you plan to grow your business?
- Do you have an exit plan?
- Do you have the right resources to meet your goals, objectives, vision, etc.?

(2) Finances

This section is meant for individuals who are starting a new business or funding a new product or service.

Make My Brand Bigger

Many companies fail due to the lack of a sound financial structure. It is paramount for every new brand to document where the funds will come from and how they will be spent. It is easy to procrastinate and put this off for another day. I implore you to take a moment and think about how you will fund your rebrand or launch a new brand. There are plenty of accountants out there to help you organize your finances and develop a sound strategy. As a small business owner myself, I know the earlier you secure and tackle your financial structure the better.

In the past, I have heard many times, "Money is the fuel for a business." If you are a business owner or manage the finances for a company, you understand how important this is. If you don't have a well-defined financial plan, the likelihood of your success diminishes greatly.

Plus, not only will you need secure financial support during the initial launch, you will need the appropriate funds to get you through the post-launch phase. And, a good financial plan will provide you with a better understanding of your expected cash burn rate.

TIP: Make a detailed list of where the money is coming from to fund your business. This list might include investors, family, friends, rich uncle, etc. Also, make sure you have secured your finances prior to any spending.

Discovery and Gap Analysis

(3) Timeline

Setting the timeline includes gathering information from everyone involved and understanding all of the moving parts to successfully launch your brand. Keep in mind, a timeline is also critical if you are currently in a rebrand initiative. The timeline to unveil your brand should consist of a predefined launch date, when the product or service will be ready for the public, printing or manufacturing deadlines, employee and vendor resources, sales team needs, marketing schedule, etc.

Below are general guidelines you can follow to establish a sound timeline:

- Create an outline of your tentative timeline as early as possible in your plan.
- Anticipate there may be steps in your timeline where there will be issues. In this case, allow yourself several days to weeks of extra time.
- As my mother used to say, "Do your homework." This will help you understand each step or phase of your timeline.
- Don't hesitate to consult with professionals.
- Take your internal team into consideration. Ask them for a reasonable timeline to get their part of the work completed.

Timing is everything. Review your calendar and carefully map out your significant milestones. Your timeline should be very detailed. More often than not, you will run into scheduling issues and events that will undoubtedly shift or change your timeline. Try to anticipate them and add extra time where necessary.

TIP: If you are looking to get a strong reaction from your potential customers and the media, plan on a week-long launch and put an exorbitant amount of energy into your brand launch.

(4) Key Players

At this point, you have begun to gather pertinent business information such as business objectives, finances, and timelines. Let's not forget to also make a list of key players and their responsibilities. Understanding who your key players are is essential on several levels.

You will need to know exactly who the various stakeholders are and what roles they will play in the brand launch. Mainly, who is responsible for what task? Getting buy-in and final approval from the right people will help streamline the process and alleviate confusion.

You may find the following questions helpful in defining the key players, resources, and additional support.

Discovery and Gap Analysis

Executives/Key Players:
- What roles do you currently have in place?
- What roles need to be filled now and in the future?
- Who are the primary decision makers?
- Are there clear and designated responsibilities for everyone involved?

Resources, Support, and Financial Partnerships:
- Are there support resources in place such as vendors and employees who can help?
- Do you have all necessary legal issues addressed such as clearance, ownership, protection, and contractual terms?
- After deciding on outside resources, what are their roles? And have you clearly defined them with your team?
- Are there any financial partnerships? Silent, angel investors, friends, and family?

Finally, full transparency of who the primary decision makers are will help streamline overall communications and efficiency.

Not too long ago, we finished a rebrand initiative for a technology company. At the beginning of each brand engagement, part of our process is to identify the key players. This usually takes the form of actively asking who will be involved and who will make the final decisions. As we sat down to discuss various aspects of the technology company's business and the challenges specific to their brand, we were introduced to the owner and two other senior employees. Throughout the discussion, they assured us they were the only individuals making decisions. So, for the next several months we proceeded with an enormous amount of work and captured amazing feedback throughout the process. At each step we meticulously revealed, discussed, analyzed, and eventually made great progress in uncovering the true brand message, position, brand essence, etc. We redefined their brand message and integrated it into their overall brand story.

As we were getting ready to wrap up the rebrand initiative, we scheduled a final meeting to review all of the work completed so far and discuss how the new brand was going be implemented (relaunched). A young woman entered the room and quietly sat down. I introduced myself and she did so in return. "Hi, I'm the owner's wife and I wanted to hear about the rebrand." This seemed innocent enough until the second slide of the presentation where we reviewed the central point of the brand, the brand essence. We began to hear comments from the owner's wife: "I don't like it." "I'm unclear as to what that means." "How did you come to that conclusion?"

Several minutes later, which seemed like an eternity, I decided it would be wise to hold off on the subsequent brand discussion. I politely asked if she would like us to review the past data along with the reason behind each of the brand decisions we made as a team. I then proceeded to go back several months into our previous discussions, along with the detailed data we had acquired and outlined every point, every milestone, and every decision made by the senior team. When it was all said and done, she loved the direction and everything turned out well. Although I wish the owner had been transparent with everyone that his wife would be involved in making final decisions.

Important side note about key players: Full transparency matters. Branding projects are very time consuming, and there are many milestones in making major decisions about the direction of the brand and strategic plans. The decisions made at each milestone are critical and shape future decisions. If your co-worker, boss, wife, husband, or significant other plays a major role in making decisions, it should be transparent to everyone involved from the very beginning. And they should be included in all meetings so they can gain the pertinent insights about the brand and help you make better decisions along the way.

TIP: Make a list of all resources you will need, internal and external, and identify the missing gaps.

2.2 Legal Assistance for Brand Clearance, Ownership, and Protection

Setting up a detailed legal strategy that covers your business needs and also helps to protect your investment is one of the most critical aspects of a healthy brand. While it goes without saying, ensuring that you have the legal right to use a name or a specific product without infringing on someone else's intellectual property rights is critical to the long-term success of your business.

There are many naming strategies you can follow and there are plenty of intellectual property attorneys to provide you with guidance. Irrespective of the legal conundrum you may face with your brand name, there is a general guiding rule that not only makes a strong brand strategy, but is founded on common sense: Do not use general industry terms for your brand name.

Some time ago we were hired to help a struggling national media company. They provide unique and one-off events streamed into local theaters. For instance, if there

Discovery and Gap Analysis

is a major event in New York, they stream the event live to select theaters throughout the country. Therefore, people in Denver, Colorado would have the opportunity to see the event streamed live.

After several months of discovery, working through their brand and identifying key issues, we concluded one of the major problems was grounded in their name "Big Screen Productions." The problem with their generic name transcended throughout their company and the industry as a whole.

The first issue was the inability for them to be found online. As an example, if you were to search "big screen productions" on the Internet, you would get over 37 million hits, and most of the top hits were about "big screen" televisions and monitors. So, to get their company ranked in the first or second page for any of the search engines would take a monumental effort.

The other issue was the generic name in and of itself. It was very difficult for anyone to remember the actual name of the company.

Finally, the generic name did not instill a unique brand message. The name did not connect with people thoughtfully or emotionally.

Based on their business growth goals, we helped them

identify a name that was not only unique, but also focused on their brand's core essence and enabled them to instill the correct emotional response from their customers. "Fathom Entertainment" was born. The response, the energy, and the momentum the company gained were paramount to their success and helped them grow their business beyond their initial expectations. We also fixed other branding issues, but the renaming of the company was the central point of success. Choosing the right name takes thorough research and patience.

Once you have a name for your new brand (see the next chapter) it is wise to hire an intellectual property attorney to review and research the name for any potential infringements. When you obtain the green light to proceed, you will be able to use the name for your new brand. However, it is imperative to understand that even though you have been cleared to use your chosen name, it's important not only to ensure that you don't infringe upon another party but also that the brand itself is protectable. This should not discourage you from doing the initial search and registering your name with the United States Patent and Trademark Office (USPTO).

Besides securing your new brand name, there are other legal practices you should also have in place. These

Discovery and Gap Analysis

include legal documents such as copyrights, patents, trademarks, trade secret, and NDA's. A good attorney will help you organize and define the necessary documents, and navigate the legal process.

As you build your brand and work with third parties, it's important to ensure you own the work any third party provide to you. Take for example, when you hire a photographer to shoot photos for your brochure, the photographer—in most if not all states—owns the copyright to those images. Or let's say for example you hired a developer to code software for your company. They most likely also own the copyright for the work completed. Of course, these scenarios are challengeable in court, but no one wants to spend an exorbitant amount of time and money working through these issues. It is up to you to work through your agreement for the use of the any outside service you hire. Spend the extra time upfront to understand what services you are contracting and what can potentially give you an enormous amount of angst. Ultimately, it is important to ensure you own the work others have created for you.

TIP: There are many affordable and talented intellectual property attorneys. They will help you resolve business and intellectual property issues in advance. The timing to protect your brand is critical. Yes, it's true. The sooner you provide your attorney with the information you plan on protecting, the better they will be able to serve your needs. So, trust me, working with an attorney will be one of the best investments you will make.

Finally, if you have a set of legal documents you plan on using for your business, be sure to share them with your attorney for specific feedback.

2.3 Brand Elements

Through the discovery phase, making a list and identifying all of the necessary brand elements will shed light on the areas you need to work on the most. In this section, we are going to cover the necessary brand elements you need to define your brand.

To help you understand the context of the terminology used throughout this book, I have included a glossary with brief descriptions.

For an existing brand, it is not unusual to have several of these brand elements already in place. If so, these can be used to formulate a foundation for the elements we already know to be true. And just because you have some of the brand elements in place, it does not mean you should consider them as final. Many times, when we work with clients on the initial discovery phase, we consider existing

Discovery and Gap Analysis

brand elements and find many to be a solid starting point.

But just as often, we discover brand elements that are not a good representation of the current brand. If you are planning on rebranding, identifying these brand elements early in the process will help you establish a strong foundation and define where your gaps may be.

It is very important to have all of the brand elements clearly defined before launching your brand. I believe it is crucial to have a strong brand foundation and a clear understanding of your brand. When you work through these brand elements, you will uncover key brand attributes that eventually play an important role in your external marketing. Not only will this help you to precisely tell your brand story, explain your brand promise, and communicate how you differ from your competitors, it will also help you avoid spending money on unsuccessful campaigns and less-than-optimal advertising.

Understanding your brand and creating a robust strategy to promote it will make the difference between success and failure.

In the past, I have shared a simple graph with my clients (see Figure 1) to help them visualize the various brand elements and how they work with a brand initiative. Take note of the two major areas, the internal and the external brand considerations. The internal brand elements are meant to help you define your brand's "Secret Sauce." The external brand elements define the primary branding execution and strategic focus.

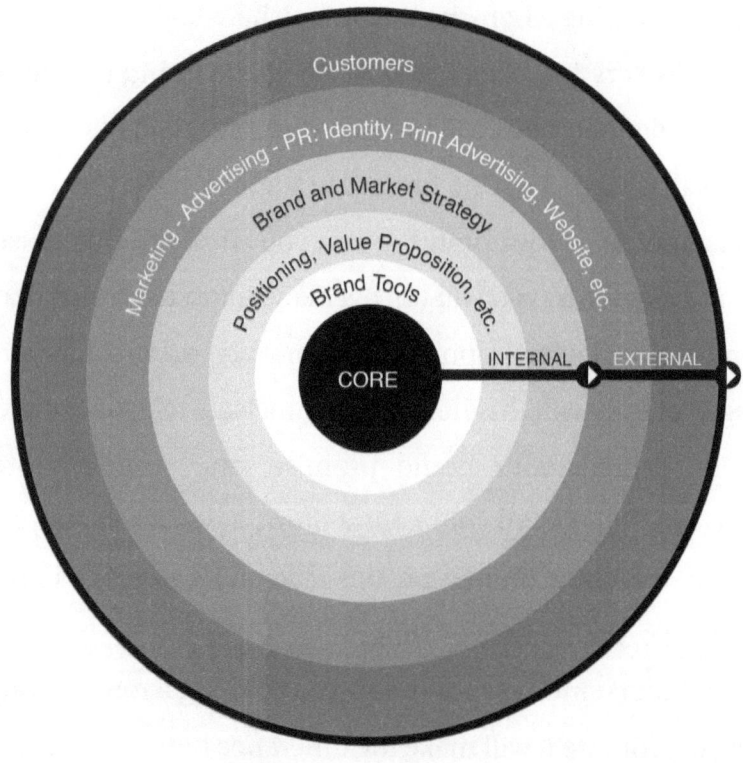

Figure 1

When identifying the gaps in the brand elements, what you have and don't have may indeed be a little challenging at first. After spending time identifying your gaps, you will

Discovery and Gap Analysis

have a better understanding of how much work you need to do to get your brand clearly defined and completed.

TIP: I often ask my clients to jot down a brief description of their business and then separately write down a description of their products or services. There is no right or wrong way to do this. This exercise may involve several refinements. The goal is to define your company clearly, and to define the products or services the company provides in a straightforward and easy-to-understand statements. While these initial descriptions will not literally be used for marketing, this exercise will help you begin to create a contextual foundation. It will also be used to further describe and identify other brand elements in future phases. Naturally, the descriptions should be written in your own words and will assist in building the foundation for your brand.

To help organize your thoughts, I have listed a series of questions that eventually need to be answered. Review them and decide what you currently have in place and what needs to be developed further. We will explain these in more detail in the following chapter "Brand Building."

TIP: Make a list of what you have and don't have. If you are not sure, mark it on your list as a to-do.

Fundamentally, as you work through the gaps in your brand, these questions will help you define and build your brand's "Secret Sauce." It might be too early to have the answers to all of these questions. Reviewing these early in the process will help you understand the gaps in your brand.

- How can you briefly describe your company, products, and services?
- Have you defined your brand personality and character?
- Do you have a brand promise?
- Do you have a value proposition? If I give you a dollar, what will you give me in exchange?
- What is your brand essence? This is the main core of the brand.
- What are your business values and how do they impact your brand?
- What position does your brand occupy in the market compared to your competitors?
- What specifically differentiates your brand from your competitors?
- What kind of tone does your brand emit?
- What is your brand story? This focuses on the narrative and prompts action.
- What is your brand message? This is about the company features, value proposition, and how you position your brand.

Discovery and Gap Analysis

All of these brand elements will also become essential in the development of your marketing and sales strategies and tactics.

TIP: Don't skip this important planning step. Being patient while building your brand is essential to your success. Many people jump right into the design of their logo before fully understanding their brand, their position in the market, who their customers are, who their segmented markets are, and what separates them from their competitors. They try to prematurely force the contextual part of the brand into their "pretty" logo that has no real emotional connection to their true brand and ultimately, in the near future, there will be a need to update or change the logo. For most businesses, it is tremendously expensive to change a logo due to strategic missteps early in the brand building process.

Finally, and if done correctly, this exercise will provide Context, Clarity, and Meaning to your brand and your story. Again, we will delve deeper into this topic in the "Brand Building" chapter.

2.4 Marketing and Sales

At this point, you probably understand the importance of outlining the critical elements that are needed to begin uncovering your gaps. Marketing and sales play an essential part of brand building. This is also the right time for me to suggest that when you build a brand, you need to take into consideration every aspect of your company.

Marketing and sales will provide the fuel and momentum to gain market share and brand loyalty. Together, their primary focus is to increase revenue.

I often encounter situations within marketing departments where they do not talk to the sales department. It is surprising that both departments seem to only operate within their individual timelines and goals. While there are significant differences between the two departments, there are also many similarities. Business goals are the main driving force for most companies and enable a culture where both departments work together in tandem. Marketing goals and sales targets should be tackled together.

First, let's begin by understanding the difference between marketing and sales.

Marketing uses research to identify the needs of the organization's customers and promotes the brand accordingly. The marketing team is usually in charge of implementing various systems such as email integration, sales software, lead generation systems, metrics, etc. They help define which collateral is necessary for each channel and optimize their cost for an efficient return on investment

Discovery and Gap Analysis

(ROI). Marketing is also the main bridge between the basic brand elements and defining a clear brand story. They are the gatekeepers for the brand. They will help to facilitate a consistent message throughout all communication mediums such as ads, brochures, radio advertising, commercials, case studies, and so on.

Sales, in turn, are interpersonal relationships with customers. The sales team typically finds themselves in client meetings, one-on-one conversations, attending networking events, replying to emails, and taking plenty of customer and new lead calls. They close the deal.

When both of these departments work in tandem, amazing things happen. The marketing team can provide brand guidance along with strategic and tactful suggestions to win more business with the sales team. The sales team can also provide ground-level feedback from their existing customers about the brand. Their feedback is critical information for the marketing team to absorb so they can make necessary communication adjustments.

For example, the sales team may have heard from several of their customers that they love the way a particular capability works within one of their products. The marketing department can use this information to brag about their capability in the form of a testimonial or case study and help promote the brand. Or, let's say the sales team has received feedback the product does not perform as well as advertised. This information can be passed to the marketing department for them to review their brand promise and it can also be passed to the manufacturing or the development team for refinement.

Marketing by nature helps to nurture leads. Sales teams close the deal.

Keep in mind every business is different. You may have two ice cream shops several blocks away from each other and there will be significant differences between the two companies. Just like branding, marketing, and sales for each business also vary considerably. You cannot integrate a single strategic template and apply it to all.

The sole purpose of the following exercise is to identify and eventually create tools that are pertinent to the success of your business. They are designed to ask critical questions about the current status of your marketing and sales.

Remember, when these tools are created and executed, the sales team will be able to efficiently use the strong brand story, brand message, positioning, and many more brand elements to empower them to close the deal.

Within the discovery and gap analysis, determine what elements of marketing and sales are in place, what

Discovery and Gap Analysis

needs to be considered further, and what needs to be built.

Integration of a new marketing strategy takes plenty of resources, time and money. It is important to begin laying out a rough idea of your marketing plan during the discovery phase. As you formulate your brand strategy, details should become clearer as to what you should implement to meet your goals and objectives.

The following questions are designed to help you begin to identify areas to consider in your marketing and sales plan.

- Have you researched and do you understand your potential customers?
- Do you have past customer surveys or data you can use to understand your markets?
- Have you identified your current customers? (Profiles, personas, segmentation, trends, etc.)
- Do you clearly understand and can you identify your primary competitors?
- How well do you know your competitors? What is their positioning, marketing and selling strategy, their revenue and market share?
- Do you have a distribution plan? How are you going to get your product or service into the hands of your prospective buyers?

Make My Brand Bigger

- What does the current market look like for your products and services?
- Do you have or need a sales team?
- Do you have an established sales and marketing budget? This coincides with your company information and your overall company finances.
- Have you created a SWOT Analysis? (Strengths, Weakness, Opportunities, Threats)
- Have you secured your online social media accounts with your company, service, and product name? These include accounts such as Facebook, Twitter, and Instagram.
- Finally, have you researched the available domain names for your brand? It is highly unlikely you will find your brand name available as a dotcom domain extension. The availability of a top tier domain name should be taken into consideration when contemplating a new name. Although, it is my opinion, the top domain extensions, that is, .com, .biz, .net, are mostly irrelevant anymore, as long as you can get alternative domain extensions. Finally, through your research, if the chosen domains cause infringement rights, look to your attorney for guidance.

Discovery and Gap Analysis

2.5 Visual Brand Audit

The visual brand elements communicate a lot about your brand. These elements consist of your logo, company colors, font usage, textures, photography style, and most importantly the consistency of all of these visual brand elements through out your marketing and sales communications.

This exercise is primarily for an existing brand, although it is good to review this section and get a great understanding of how you might apply these techniques to your new brand. Plus, after launching your new brand, you should periodically apply this exercise to your brand as a way to stay in line with your short and long-term goals.

First, find a suitable location to lay out every piece of marketing and communications materials for your business. Place them categorically in sections: ads, website banner ads, Facebook ads, brochures, trade show pamphlets, catalogs, etc. Spread the pieces out so you can visually see all of them.

Once you have them laid out, you should review the consistency of how the visual elements are treated.

For example, more often than not, when we conduct this exercise we find major issues with how the brand is expressed. These might include the use of inconsistent photography style, or the use of numerous fonts on a single advertisement, and to add to the complexity, different fonts being used throughout all communication materials. Ironically, sometimes companies get complacent even in their use of their logo. Many times, after conducting a visual brand audit, we find major issues with varying colors, fonts, and the placement of the logo mark, etc. These are all areas that should be tightened up and integrated into a brand standard guide.

Finally, review all of these communication materials and begin to make a list of necessary modifications or changes in order of priority. Take on the easier challenges first, then tackle the more complex visual brand issues later. It is not uncommon to engage with a branding firm to help you figure out the best to way fix complex issues and visually express your brand properly.

Remember, brand consistency is key to building brand equity.

The following questions are designed to gather fundamental brand consistency input from your team.

- Is the logo usage consistent throughout?
- Do we have a set of designated colors we are using for our brand? How can we standardize them?
- Are the various photographs consistent? Do they

Discovery and Gap Analysis

convey the brand's culture and do they connect with our customers?
- How many font styles are we using? Can we define a primary and secondary font and stick to it?
- What is the main message of each piece? Does it line up with our brand story and message?
- What is our call-to-action on each piece?
- Have we differentiated ourselves from our competitor, and if so, how?

What's next?

Once you have completed your visual brand audit, gather your closest competitor's communication materials and lay them out next to yours. This additional exercise will provide valuable information for differentiation.

Several months ago, we worked with a national software company to help them with a rebrand initiative.

While we were conducting this exercise, we noticed there were a lot of visual brand similarities between them and their competitors. The initial feedback we received from their senior team was that they loved their current look and feel. After conducting several more research-based exercises, we came to the conclusion their visual brand was too close to their competitors. Therefore, causing confusion in the marketplace which negated any brand loyalty or brand equity they were trying to gain.

After some initial pushback to change their look, we decided it was best to provide a visual brand exercise explicitly focusing on one aspect of their marketing strategy. We took several ads and placed them on a board for everyone to see. There were five ads; four from different competitors and one from their company. We placed a sticky note over each of the logos and asked if they could identify the ads that belonged to each company. There was an awkward silence and then one of the senior team members for the company said, "I get it now. We have become a generic company. We have not created a unique visual preference and people don't know who we are." This was groundbreaking and a major milestone was accomplished in the further development of their existing brand. We then proceeded to update their brand with the use of a unique industry color and fonts that reflected their tone and culture, and photography treatment that was both unique to the industry and connected well with their customers.

Overall, your visual communication materials should be a distinctive and a strong representation of your unique brand.

2.6 Wrap Up

We have reviewed a great amount of information to help determine what you need to analyze your brand gaps.

Overall, be diligent. Gather the information you need to truly understand your brand and fill in the gaps.

Company Detail TIP

Take time to write out a description of your company along with descriptions of your products and services. This will enable you to understand your business more clearly.

Brand Elements TIP

Be patient when building your brand. Write out and share your brand details with your team for feedback before designing the logo or defining the brand colors. The attention to detail and overall buy-in from your team will save you a significant amount of time and money later on in the process.

Marketing and Sales TIP

If you have not done so already, develop a SWOT analysis. This is a detailed list of your Strengths, Weaknesses, Opportunities, and Threats. It will help clarify the necessary elements of your marketing and sales strategy as well as help define your brand position. The SWOT analysis is an extremely valuable tool that will provide you with additional information to be used in other areas of your brand development.

Competition TIP

Fully understand who your top 4-5 competitors are and what makes them unique. Compare their brand promise, value proposition, brand message, etc. against yours. Alternatively, the most significant mistake you could make is to build a brand that does not differentiate from your competitors, therefore not creating a preference for your brand.

Sales Process TIP

Have you mapped out your customer journey? How do your clients find and interact with your brand? What type of experience do you want your customers to have?

Legal Strategy Tip

It is critical to initiate the legal protection for your brand early in the process; otherwise, all of your efforts might prove to be a complete waste of time.

Finally, understand no two businesses are alike. You may need to delve deeper into certain areas of these exercises to get a more complete picture of your brand.

CHAPTER THREE

What's in a Name

Choosing the right name for your new brand usually takes a great deal of time, research, and deep soul searching. The amount of stress involved is similar to coming up with a name for your new baby. And in reality, a new brand is a lot like a new family member. You'll live with a brand for a long time.

Positioning, a clear articulation of the brand, its unique offerings, and the competitive landscape are just a few main factors to take into consideration when choosing a new brand name. The right name should help differentiate you from your competitors, increase brand equity, and create a strong brand preference.

Make My Brand Bigger

The following list includes the Top Ten Lessons I have learned working on brand name initiatives.

Lesson 1. Become a Pioneer

One of the biggest mistakes companies make is choosing a name that does not differentiate them from their competition. Sometimes, the general attitude seems to involve not wanting to take a risk, which is entirely the opposite of a correct naming strategy. Taking a chance and becoming a pioneer in your industry is what will set you apart and provide differentiation between you and your competitors.

When choosing a name, it is essential to connect with your customers. So, an early clarification of several brand elements may be in order. These clarifications include definitions of your brand essence, brand character, brand position, brief company description, positioning in the marketplace, etc. Your trademark name is what creates an association between you and your customers and becomes your primary identifier.

Lesson 2. I Am Who I Am

Once you have selected a short list of names for your company, product, or service, it is important to research these names using tools such as Google, Bing, and Yahoo to find out how much "noise" there may be with any of the possible name choices. The "noise" refers to the number of "hits" each name gets from the Internet search. This exercise should provide you with enough information to make a calculated analysis of the initial risks involved.

This search should not be used as a definitive evaluation of your risks. Hiring an intellectual property attorney will help to refine your short list and enable you to resolve the uncertainties that are apparent in advance. Also, timing is always critical. Put another way, if someone else has already begun using your name, or one very similar to it, they can endlessly assert their rights and interfere with your long-term business plans. Your ability to be the first one on the block to use a particular name for a specific product or service is monumentally crucial.

Lesson 3. You Are at War

Your new name says a lot about your brand. Your competitors will notice and most likely make future decisions based on the market threat or lack thereof. It is essential to do an initial brand study to include your competitors. It is easy to forget when launching or re-launching a new company, product, or service that you are competing for a market share. Research how your competitors describe themselves, how they are positioned in the market, and study the names used in that industry for trends. These topics, along with other factors, should provide you with beneficial information on name usage and how to best compete within your industry.

Lesson 4. Leave a Legacy

Using your given name, such as Smith Inc., may or may not be a good choice. It is essential to look forward one, three, and ten years from now. Even though there are naming professionals who suggest using your name as the best way to go, I believe using your name may, in all actuality, create a multitude of complex issues further down the road. These complex issues can include selling your company to a prospective buyer or forming a partnership. Alternatively, consider the overall fact that your last name may not be such a good choice for the overall benefit of the brand and what it stands for.

Furthermore, if your company's brand is seen as an "personal" brand as opposed to a "business" brand, you may have trouble selling it. My recommendation is to add your name to the list of potential brand names, but be objective about the pros and cons. The outcome will be a more thought-out and strategic solution.

Lesson 5. My Exit Plan Before I Start

Many people start a business and don't consider what they would like to do with it once they are done. Provide yourself ample time to think about what you would ultimately like to do with the new company, product, or service when you are ready to retire or move on to another venture. Would you like to sell the business, merge with another company, engage in a partnership, or create a system of junior partners who will eventually take over? These are essential questions to consider in advance.

Lesson 6. My Domain

Once you have chosen a short list of names and researched the domain names, the likelihood of the selected names being available for use is usually pretty slim. Although, if you find yourself in a situation that your desired name is available as a .com, .net, or whichever your preference is, make sure to secure it immediately. Don't wait, as someone else might secure it before you do. This does not mean it is an immediate deal killer. You can creatively add words to the front or back of the brand name to acquire a unique and strong domain name that sets the brand apart. The process of creating a strong domain name that fits your chosen company name can take some time and research.

However, remember it is always important to keep the domain name as short as possible.

Lesson 7. Get Off My Cloud!

There may be many situations where you have done everything right only to find out that someone has already claimed your chosen name. My suggestion is that you don't immediately fire off a hasty letter of cease and desist until you have done some additional research. Timing is everything. It is unnecessary to sue everyone you think might be infringing on your rights. In cases where someone truly is encroaching on the rights you have established, first make sure you have done all of your homework. Only then take a stand and notify the other party. However, I strongly recommend hiring an intellectual property attorney to assist you in sorting out your best options.

Lesson 8. Change is Good *Sometimes*

Every now and then you might contemplate changing your company, product, or service name. Although this is a very complicated question to answer, some key identifiers help provide the initial clues as to whether or not you should move ahead. These include competitors using a similar name, major core brand changes, the current name not getting marketing traction, and legal issues to name a few. These and other factors may be triggers that solicit initial conversations on whether or not you should make a name change. I recommend hiring an outside brand consultant who is familiar with these topics to help guide you and provide various options.

Lesson 9. Protect Your Investment

A trademark attorney rarely becomes involved in the process of selecting the proper brand message or brand story you will ultimately use. This is the purview of marketing and branding experts. A good trademark attorney, however, is essential to ensure that you can establish rights of the chosen brand name, to undertake the process of obtaining formal protection for the name, and to enforce these rights against others.

The monetary investment most companies make for their initial launch is enormous. Not to mention the time and energy the team will invest in the new brand. Building a brand typically involves a very strategic plan and can take some time to get traction in the marketplace. Because the stakes are high, some preemptive work by a seasoned professional such as an intellectual property attorney can help you avoid major mistakes.

Lesson 10. So, What's in a Good Name?

Finally, the right name should be unique to your industry, memorable and legally protectable. Also, a good name should define the uniqueness of your brand and speak to the brand essence of the company.

CHAPTER FOUR

Brand Building

Let's start brand building!

In this chapter on Brand Building and defining your brand's "Secret Sauce," we will cover the foundation of your brand elements in more detail. We will describe each element and provide examples of how they will help build your brand and your unique story.

Developing a robust brand strategy can be one of the most challenging steps in the marketing plan process. It is often the biggest challenge for most businesses, but it is an integral step in creating a compelling brand. Typically, I challenge our clients to wrestle with what their organization truly stands for and what makes them valuable to their customers. Through several workshops, we ask them to think about how they are seen today, who they aspire to be, and who their customers want them to be.

A quick note about what a brand is: Historically, no one really knows for sure how the terminology "brand" came to be. Some people speculate the obvious: the branding of animals to identify who owns the animal, such as a farmer branding his cattle to identify the ownership of his herd.

A brand is not just a logo. A brand is the intuitive and emotional feelings your customer has with your brand.

The reason it's so hard for most people to define a brand is because a brand is not tangible. Your brand lives in the mind of your customers. That is also why a brand is so difficult to define, create, and maintain.

Furthermore, a brand is developed through the accumulation of all touchpoints your brand has with your current and potential customers. This means that every point of contact with customers, partners, and suppliers is essential to building those lasting impressions—from the way you answer the phone to individual sales activities. It is crucial to deliver the right brand message and stay consistent to achieve your ultimate business goals.

Think about it this way. When you first meet someone,

you immediately begin to create an idea of them. After you have had several interactions and have spoken with them several times, your opinion about them evolves and becomes more clear and definitive.

Later, someone might ask you "What do you think about John?" At which point you might say things such as "He is a really nice guy," or "He really likes to argue," or "He seemed really busy and didn't have much time for me," or "He is brilliant." As you can imagine, these are the same intuitive and emotional feelings people have about brands. In addition, people generalize their overall opinions and come to general conclusions.

Below are several criteria we use to define a strong brand. Most importantly, they all need to be true.

- Your brand should reduce uncertainty and generate a sense of trust by association. Familiarity is key.
- Your brand must be memorable.
- Your brand must have an intuitive and emotional connection to your customers.
- Your brand must offer a unique experience.
- Your brand must answer the question, "Why?"
- Your brand must create a purpose in your consumer's life. (Help versus Sell)
- It must convey the true essence of your brand.

Make My Brand Bigger

A well-developed brand strategy provides essential resources for the marketing, advertising and communications teams to draw from without the exhaustive need to create it at every communication juncture. The consistency of a brand message has long been a factor in developing a positive perspective about your brand. A well-defined brand helps companies achieve a strong level of trust.

TIP: You may find it helpful to review the Marketing and Sales chapter prior to finalizing this section. The information gained in the Marketing and Sales chapter will help shape many decisions about your brand.

The Life Cycle of a Brand

After decades of working with brands, I found it essential to help my clients understand the cycle people go through when considering their products or services (see Figure 2). The following is a detailed explanation.

Defining the "Brand"

As we reviewed earlier, the first step is to "define the brand." This is the first phase you need to have clearly defined and created. This is your brand's "Secret Sauce." This phase is about defining the intuitive and emotional response you are trying to generate from your customers.

Brand Building

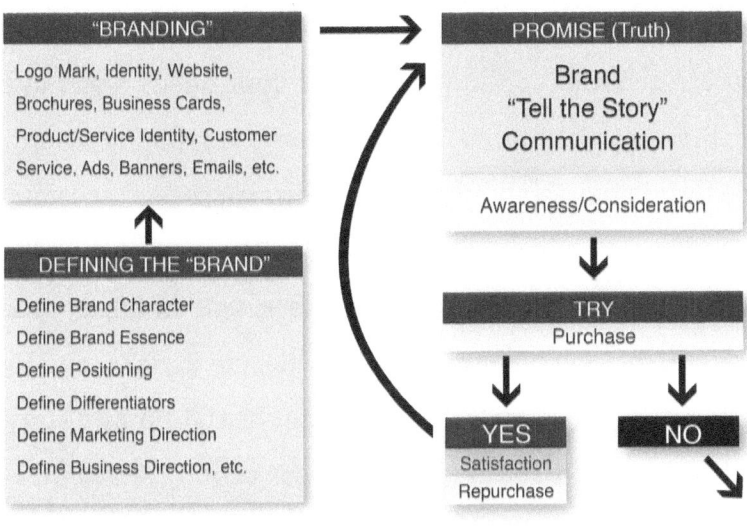

Figure 2

Branding

The second phase emphasizes the execution of the brand. In this phase, you will define all of your communications materials, identify who you are targeting, and how you will communicate your brand story and message to your customers. These are designed to provide you with tools to reach your customers through various touchpoints.

Awareness and Consideration Phase (Promise)

In this phase your brand is marketed to the world. You will have launched your brand with the right brand story and message. Keep in mind, if your customers do not know you are a viable option for meeting their needs, you have lost many opportunities. This is where good marketing and sales strategies are paramount to your success. Once your customers are aware of your product or service, this phase focuses on their consideration. Have you defined your brand to the point where your potential customer sees it as a good option to try it? Have you told the right brand story and communicated the defining areas of your brand message? IS IT COMPELLING? If you answered "yes" to all of these, then you most likely have a new customer.

Try it Phase

So, you have new customers and they have tried your product or service. This phase is probably the most important of all. Did your product or service meet your client's expectations as defined in your initial brand development phase? Did you deliver on your brand promise?

Conclusion Phase

Now, if you answered "no," then you will most likely lose that customer. They may say terrible things about your product or service. If you answered "yes" to the preceding phase, then you are on your way to a successful business.

With every new happy customer, you will most likely have a repeat customer. Also, every new happy customer will share their experience with confirmation of your brand promise. Furthermore, note the curved arrow pointing upwards from the "satisfied" customer to the brand promise. This indicates that although customers are satisfied, they will always look for confirmation as to whether or not they made the right decision. This is reinforced through your efforts of engaging them through feedback questionnaires, speaking directly with them, brand loyalty programs, advertisements, coupons, etc.

TIP: Make sure your promise to your customer is something you can deliver upon. You don't have to be the first, the best, or the newest to be successful. There are many great brands that provide products or services which are not any of the aforementioned. What they do best is provide a unique experience and deliver on their brand promise.

4.1 Brand Purpose

Consumers have an uncanny ability to quickly read into a company's brand and decide whether the product or service is right for them. Most brands have a predefined purpose and do a terrible job communicating that purpose to their prospective customers.

Make My Brand Bigger

Communicating the purpose of a brand is the pinnacle of how one might decide if the product or service offering is right for them or not. The brand purpose is directly connected to the needs of the consumer. A simple question every brand should ask and answer is, "What is the purpose of my brand? And why are we in this business?" The answer is usually derived from delving into many other aspects of the brand. The brand purpose is often defined at the conclusion of a brand research initiative. The brand purpose should be straightforward, unique and specific. Some examples: "To provide the world with a unique, refreshing drink"—Coca-Cola, "To design and produce a vehicle that is very safe to drive"—Volvo, "To change the way people interact with technology for a better life experience"—Apple. These conclusions may seem obvious, although it is often a very difficult conclusion for many businesses to define.

Understanding the purpose of your brand will have a significant impact on your overall profit. Every day we are given multiple opportunities to engage with various brands. And many times we will make intuitive and quick decisions on whether to use these brands. A strong brand strategy, and a clear communication of your brand's purpose, motivates your employees to understand the purpose of your brand and results in better customer engagement.

Brand Building

Your customers will be able to understand how your brand can help them, therefore building trust and loyalty. The most successful brands understand the importance of clearly defining their brand's purpose and communicating it in a unique and simple way. Your prospective customers will most likely choose one brand over another based on how precisely the brand communicates its purpose, therefore providing a personal brand experience.

Never underestimate the power of a succinct and well-defined brand purpose. It will affect all other brand communication elements such as positioning, differentiation, and most importantly your bottom line.

As I mentioned before, the process of branding can be complicated and sometimes difficult to execute. Branding is a necessity and its sole purpose is to support all marketing efforts. Branding is one of the most critical aspects of your business. Brands are not built overnight. It takes time to build that vital reputation and connection between your company and your customers.

We all know it's not enough to have a great offering which serves a unique purpose. What many companies lack is the ability to communicate their brand's value efficiently in a clear and concise way. Your customers' actions are both emotional and rational. Companies that have defined a clear brand purpose, message, and a unique position in the marketplace are more likely to succeed. If your brand does not elicit an emotional response, then it is most likely doomed to fail.

There are several other factors of brand building that should be considered. These include lack of trust and awareness. These factors can be overcome by reinforcing your brand with consistent brand messaging and visual communications in the form of style and tone. The consistency of your brand's value and visual communications creates trust and captures the attention of your customers so they can identify and connect with the purpose of your brand. These are great ways to build confidence, reinforce the brand purpose as well as the value your brand provides.

In summary, inspiring action from your customers is crucial to the success of your brand. Understanding your brand and its purpose are monumental in helping you define your story and your message to customers. So, the next time you shop at your favorite store or use one of your favorite products, ask yourself what drove you to take action?

4.2 Brand Character and Personality

Companies often fear that their brand is elusive and undefined. The character of your brand is based on the accumulation of all touchpoints. Your competitors may be missing this very crucial step. They are typically too concerned about promoting their capabilities and often forget to integrate a well-defined brand character and personality into their communications. Your company must identify its own brand character and personality in order to successfully market to your target audience.

Think about the various brands you are currently using. Each brand has a character and personality. Some are profoundly more unique and memorable, while others are simply plain and boring. For example, the experience you have at Sam's Club differs greatly from Nordstrom. The experience you have at McDonald's differs greatly from Red Robin. What do these companies have in common? In comparison to other brands, they have defined their brand character and personality and have executed it throughout their overall customer brand experience.

People respond well to character and charisma—not so much to sales pitches. Great branding evokes an emotional response on a very personal level. The potential customer will be inspired to try your brand through a compelling desire or an urgent need.

At the same time, successful campaigns are designed to help tell the story of your unique brand. By defining your brand's character and personality, your company comes alive and engages with your customers.

When working to define your company's Brand Character, imagine that your company is a person. What would its demeanor be? Calm? Smart? Friendly? Be sure to take your entire organization into account—employees, work environment, client perceptions, etc.—to uncover the most accurate profile of the "person" your company embodies.

Next, let's understand your Brand Personality and bring it to life. If you were to personify your brand, would it be male or female? How old? What interests would they have? Where would they travel? What car would they drive and what job would they have?

The key here is that people connect with character and personality, not with sales pitches and boring businesses. When the brand speaks to interests similar to the buyers, it naturally compels the buyer to "befriend" and inherently trust your brand.

TIP: Begin defining your brand character by writing down descriptive words (primarily adjectives). Once you have them written down, review each word and circle the combination of words that seem to make the most sense for your new brand. Typically, I try to limit the number of descriptive words to three. These words will provide context when you begin to create your logo, primary and secondary brand colors, overall visual identity, and font usage. They will also help define what style of photography or images you should use.

4.3 The Tone

The tone of your brand will help you understand how to speak to your customers. The tone is directly aligned with your brand character and personality. This is defined by the overall brand strategy. For example, the company Booking.com produced a series of commercials with a whimsical tone and a tagline "booking dot yeah." And there is the playful tone from Service Masters with their animated commercials showing small toy figures who help to recover your burnt or flooded house. These are good examples that describe the brand tone.

For example, your brand character can be strong, smart, and timely, while your tone might be fun, intellectual, and caring. The tone is how the brand is communicated. Think about the tone your parents had with you when you were in trouble versus the tone they had when you did something superb. Every brand carries a unique tone that is communicated directly to their customers.

Once you have correctly defined the tone of your

brand, it will help you communicate with your customers smoothly and efficiently. The defined tone will be leveraged by everyone involved in communicating your brand through advertising, blogs, photos, graphics, etc. It is crucial to get this right and ensure it is well aligned with your overall brand strategy.

4.4 Brand Essence

What is the one word that comes to mind when you think of Volvo? How about Apple? FedEx?

If you answered safe, innovative and fast, then you're exactly right. These companies have clearly defined their brand essence.

A company's brand essence serves as the nucleus, or center, of every communication point. Therefore, all communications to the consumer need to be as clear and uniform as possible. The brand essence is the keyword that consumers associate with a company, service, or product.

A strong brand needs a good foundation at its center. In other words, every great brand has a well-defined brand essence at its core.

Most of the time, the brand essence is uncovered after thorough research into the brand. In order to arrive at the true definition of the brand essence, you must consider all aspects of your brand, including your existing messaging and correct positioning, your competitors messaging, as well as the perceptions of your customers, employees, and leaders of the company.

Let's dig a little deeper into what brand essence is. It is the central core of your brand and your business. While other brand elements can change throughout time, the brand essence should never change. The brand essence is the main reason you created your company. It is the reason you are willing to invest time, money, energy, and sometimes even your life savings into the company. This is the reason you get up in the morning and go to work.

Ultimately, the core brand essence should be described in one or two words. All of the other brand elements are specifically designed to support it.

For instance, we recently finished a project for a local dentist. We uncovered the company's brand essence as "improved health." The process to get to where we could articulate the brand essence clearly, took several months of research. We looked into various areas of the business including past history and in-depth discussions about why the company was formed. This articulation of the brand essence was critical because it helped them bring clarity to the reason why the company was operating. Employees and customers were much more engaged once we used the brand message in various internal and external communications. The brand essence is a launching point for future messaging and visuals.

The core brand essence should not be confused with positioning, which we will talk about shortly.

When should you begin thinking about your brand essence? The brand essence is typically not very obvious at the beginning of the brand discovery phase. As you work through various elements, it should become more evident. So, it is sometimes worthwhile to wait until you are close to the end of the process before you tackle this task.

The value of the brand essence is twofold. It helps to streamline the central brand story and encourages consistent brand messages at all touchpoints. And this gives way to a unique and memorable brand.

When uncovered and communicated, your brand essence should meet these crucial requirements:
- Rings true every time
- Appears in various forms of all communications
- Emerges as highly evident to the audience
- Outlasts the test of time

Remember – a strong brand starts with a strong core (the essence). It may take a lot of work to get there, but discovering the sweet spot is definitely worth the work.

4.5 Brand Values

Brand values are beneficial to brand building. These values are basically a collection of high priority statements that explain how you will treat others. These values are typically in line with your company values. They are the guiding light that helps you define how you will conduct your business. Your company values are also your brand values. Carefully consider how you are going to treat your employees and your customers, and how you will deal with various business issues.

Brand values are typically defined in a series of 3-5 words. These values should align with all other brand elements and work together to create a complete picture of your brand.

As an example, the following is a short list of brand values. You might consider these or create your own values based on your unique brand. To keep it simple, you should only integrate a combination of 3-5 brand values for integration into your brand strategy. Your brand values should be shared with your employees as a way to help them understand the importance of how they will be treated and how they should treat your customers.

- **Client-focused:** We listen, ask questions, and see issues from our client's perspective.
- **Team-oriented:** We collaborate with clients and work with internal and external teams to ensure that our clients have the solutions they require.
- **Respect:** We respect our client's vision, culture, ideas, and budget. We respect each other's talents, roles and responsibilities.
- **Creative and Innovative:** We track current and future trends, think "out of the square," then select those solutions that meet our client's needs.
- **Process-oriented:** We have well-developed processes that enable us to deliver quality work on time and within budget.
- **Pride:** We have pride in our company, our customers, and our work.
- **Self-motivated:** We are motivated by the challenge and the opportunity to work for a great company.
- **Integrity:** We are honest and trustworthy. We say what we'll do, and we do what we say.

4.6 Differentiators

We often speak about "differentiators" when defining a brand. In branding terms, a differentiator determines what brand qualities separate your brand from your competitor's brand. While a differentiator clearly states the difference between you and your competitor, it is not always the primary reason prospective clients choose you over your competitors.

Let's take a look at two definitions. First, "difference" is a point or the way in which people or things are not the same. Second, "unique" is being the only one of its kind: unlike anything else. So, if you are in charge of either building a brand or helping to redefine an existing brand, the ultimate goal should be a "unique" brand. This is partially accomplished through the combination of your brand differentiators.

In today's competitive environment, it's not enough to be different. Many companies rely solely on being different from their competitors, which is a fundamental mistake. The key issue is whether creating a difference provides enough intrigue and preference for your customers to choose your company over your competitors. By default, most companies are different anyway. So, uncovering the difference through a series of brand strategy techniques is a good start but should not be the final means on which the brand hangs its hat.

Furthermore, there needs to be a thorough investigation into what differentiates your brand from all of your competitors. And more importantly, what makes your brand "unique." This requires a comprehensive insight into the various brand elements and a clear articulation of the brand. Only then can there be a clear and concise description of the uniqueness of the brand that is easy to communicate and share.

As you work through the positioning of your brand (see next the chapter), define the primary differentiators that compel your customers to choose you over the competition. These are used to support the position in which your company is placing a stake. You may need to revisit your brand position as you uncover additional details from your competitors and predefined differentiators. Remember, the sole purpose of defining the differentiators is to support the brand position with three main points. The combination of these three points should be unique, true, profoundly defining, and purposeful.

In conclusion, understanding the "uniqueness" of your brand and executing a robust communication strategy are key to creating a memorable and unique brand that also defines a clear preference over your competitors.

How do differentiators come in to play?

While you are working to position your brand in the market, you should define why someone would choose your product or service over your competitors. These are called your differentiators. Basically, as stated previously, your differentiators separate you from the competition.

Below are several tips for uncovering the differentiators for your brand.

Gather a list of your leading competitors and research their main selling and talking points. Go to their website, Google their name or go to their store. Ask your customers what they think about company XYZ. Check their press releases. Check social media sites such as LinkedIn, Facebook and Twitter to find out what people are saying about them.

Separate the top main talking points from each of the competitors. Once you have a completed list, compare those to your new brand offerings. Are they similar? If there is no differentiation, you will need to refine your position in the marketplace.

It is crucial to understand what separates your brand and why someone would have a preference for your brand over your competitors.

Make My Brand Bigger

How many differentiators should you consider?

I typically suggest using the top three differentiators to support the positioning statement. If you are formulating a strong position in the marketplace, you should be able to support that position through unique differentiators. And by focusing on three differentiators, which are of great importance to your brand message, these will ultimately help you be more clear about your brand message and story.

Besides the aforementioned, there are several added benefits to defining your brand's differentiators. First, the differentiators set a hierarchy for how you will communicate your brand promise. Second, they are defining points for you to add clarity to your communications. Third, by defining these top three differentiators, you will be consistent with the benefits of your brand. Fourth, they will provide direct and clear talking points for your marketing and sales strategies. And finally, they will help you win and retain business by creating a point of clarity as to why customers should choose your brand over others.

The following is an example of three differentiators from a company we recently rebranded. The company's main industry is commercial real estate. They had a hard time defining the clear difference between their company and their competitors, therefore creating an atmosphere

Brand Building

of non-preference. After careful deliberation of their competitor's brand messages and in conjunction with the company's top differentiators (what makes them unique), we came up with a strong brand strategy using these top three key phrases throughout their communications.

A Commercial Real Estate Business:

Control of business

- Business expenses
- Company brand
- Growth of business
- Future of business
- Managed business expenses

More profitable (finances)

- Purchasing property is an investment
- Predictable business expenses
- Retirement planning
- Commercial real estate is a sound choice for your portfolio
- Investment is yours to keep, not the landlords

Create your own environment
- Design your own space
- Not bound by landlord
- Better image
- Better customer experience

Note: The underlined keywords and the listed supporting points for each of the main differentiators prove them to be true.

4.7 Let's Talk About POSITIONING

In the past three decades, I have read a multitude of articles about branding and positioning. They mainly focus on the end result of a strong brand position and cite taglines, which are generally used to connect with their prospective customers. What many fail to focus on are the initial critical steps necessary to develop a strong position. We will cover a fundamental positioning exercise every brand should go through.

Many marketing professionals get caught up in the nuts and bolts of running a great marketing campaign and they sometimes forget to consider the broader strategy. Positioning a brand is essential to the more extensive business strategy and helps clarify the overall branding and

Brand Building

business goals. A strong brand position is also vital because it helps drive a brand story that is meaningful, unique, and engaging. Positioning a brand should be done at various points in the life cycle of the brand. Most importantly, this exercise should be done before launching any brand. Other situations may warrant a positioning review such as market trends, new competitors, a change in the brand's capabilities, stagnant sales, new owners, new products or services added to existing lines, company expansion into different markets, etc.

Below are four steps. They will help you begin to understand where your new brand is positioned in comparison to your competitors.

1. Know your competitors

Take a look at your top competitors and make a list of their differentiators (what makes them unique and different). We touched on this previously. Do you see a trend and the differences? Are there any that stand out from the rest?

2. Define your uniqueness

Defining your uniqueness typically starts with identifying your differentiators and digging deeper to define what brand characteristics are unique to your brand.

3. Compare and contrast

Once you have defined the unique points of your brand, plot them on a graph and compare them to your top competitors. This is the basic fundamental "positioning" of your new brand (see Figure 3).

4. Position your brand for success

Plotting your brand points against those of your competitors identifies your Points of Differences (POD), and provides a clearer understanding of where your brand can honestly compete. There are also several factors that should be taken into consideration when finalizing your positioning statement. As mentioned previously, integration of your business goals, SWOT statement, understanding your brand essence, company and product description, culture, etc., should be used to help define your brand position. These are necessary, as they will offer additional insight into your unique brand and will also help establish a true and honest brand position.

Finally, a strong brand position should reflect an emotional connection between your new brand and your customer. There should be a proper balance between your new brand position and your customer's needs. The process of getting there is sometimes complicated, but the benefits of

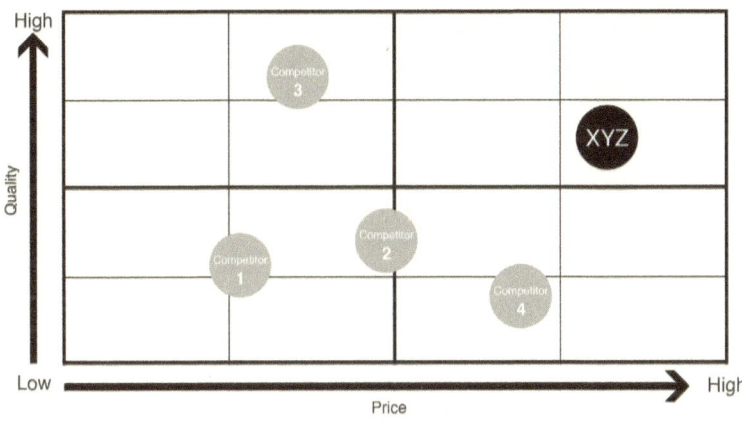

Figure 3

clearly understanding your unique brand and your customer's needs are necessary for a successful new brand launch.

Lastly, take some time to describe your brand position in a simple, yet clear paragraph. It will help you confirm whether or not you are on the right track.

How do you know if you have a strong positioning statement?

    1. Is it <u>believable</u>?
    2. Is it <u>unique</u>?
    3. Does it create an <u>emotional connection</u>?
    4. Does it meet your <u>customer's needs</u>?

If you answered "yes" to all four, then you are probably on the right track to a well-positioned brand.

4.8 Value Proposition and Brand Story

The Value Proposition

The value proposition is also one of the more critical brand elements you should define. Developing a value proposition will help you understand the basic value your brand has to your customers. First, you should set your value proposition and integrate it into your brand story. This will help determine your brand preference over your competitors. For example: think of your value proposition as what someone is willing to give you… a dollar… in exchange for your product or service. It is a promise of value you will deliver to your customers.

There are many ways to come to the conclusion of what is your value proposition. I like to use these questions as an initial guide to help wrap my mind around it:

- Does it explain how your product or service solves your customer's problem?
- What are the specific benefits associated with the use of your product or service?
- Does the value proposition clearly tell the

customer why they should buy from you?
- How is it different from my competitors?
- How much interest is there in your brand?
- Am I adding substantial value to my customer's needs?
- Can I define my value proposition in less than 15 words?
- Is the statement simple to understand?

Your value proposition does not need to answer all of these questions. They are simply designed to provide you with a starting point.

Historically, there are several companies that have developed great value propositions. These value propositions are expressed in the form of a tagline, although they are derived from tedious exploration. One example is the company Slack. They developed a productivity App designed to help people communicate more efficiently. Their value proposition is "Be more productive at work with less effort." Next let's take a look at the company Lyft. They are one of the disrupters in the taxi industry. Their value proposition is "Rides in Minutes." Then there is the giant company called Walmart, you may have heard of them. Their business model is to sell a lot of stuff at a very cheap price.

Make My Brand Bigger

Their value proposition in the form of a tagline is "Save money. Live better." Again, these companies answer the main question of why I would want to do business with them.

Although the previous examples use the tagline to convey the value proposition, it is important to note you do not always need a tagline or a slogan for your brand. There are several other ways you can express your value proposition within your marketing strategy. For instance, you could add it to your call-to-action, use it as a leading headline on a brochure, place it on your website homepage, or integrate it into your sales presentation.

Remember, your value proposition needs to be very clear and unique. Additionally, it should also be integrated into your brand story. This usually takes the form of a company description, product or service description, website copy, etc. All of these touchpoints should be designed to reinforce your brand directly.

Brand Story

Let's discuss your brand story. You are at an exciting point where you can begin defining your unique brand story. This is the phase where you begin to articulate the overall uniqueness of your brand.

Brand Building

To create a brand story, use the information from the accumulation of all the work you have completed so far. In conjunction with all of the information, you will create a meaningful story or emotion for your customers to experience. So, your brand will not be exclusively defined by your product or service—it will also be defined by your customer and their experience. Developing the right narrative takes a lot of ongoing work. Remember, you can't control all aspects of your brand story.

A great example of a brand story is Toms Shoes. If you are familiar with their brand, you have probably heard about the founder. While traveling in Argentina, he witnessed the hardship many children faced while growing up without shoes. Toms Shoes promotes their brand story as a way to differentiate themselves and provide an emotional context for the preference of their brand. Furthermore, they describe their business model as "One for One." This simply reminds people that when they purchase a pair of shoes, Toms will donate a new pair to a child in need.

Below are several questions to help you begin developing your brand story:

- What problem are you solving?
- Have you accomplished or uncovered something amazing that drove you to create the brand?

- Have you discovered a new technique, formula, product, etc.?
- Do you have a personal story about your brand?
- Is there a social issue you are trying to solve and how were you impacted by it?

Your brand story should be rooted in the purpose of your brand. It is important to note that your brand story should be true and authentic as well as memorable and unique. When creating your brand story, think about how you will deliver it through your marketing channels and how you will support it.

Let's review a few key tips we've previously covered.

TIP: Remember, for your brand character, begin by writing down descriptive words that you can use to describe your new brand. Once you have them written down, review each word and circle the combination of words that seem to make the most sense for your brand.

TIP: Regarding brand essence, your goal is to come up with a one or two-word combination that clearly defines your brand.

TIP: For a good positioning statement, these are the basic requirements.

1. Is it <u>Believable</u>?
2. Is it <u>Unique</u>?
3. Does it create an <u>Emotional Connection</u>?
4. Does it meet your <u>Customer's Needs</u>?

TIP: Now that you have finished your brand positioning, you should wait until you have all brand elements clearly defined and approved before you begin the vital process of designing your logo.

TIP: Review the details of the final summary with your senior team who are engaged throughout the process. Ask for feedback before executing any brand elements in the Marketing and Sales phases.

CHAPTER FIVE

Customer Experience (Journey)

The "Customer Experience (Journey)" is at the core of brand building. Everything you do to implement your brand affects your customer journey. Your brand is built on the customer's experience. Without a positive customer experience you don't have a sustainable brand.

Every interaction your customer has with your brand will reinforce your brand promise. The key is to align every aspect of your brand with your customer needs to create a memorable (positive) experience.

Innovation

When you consider your customer experience, take a

close look at trends and gather insights from your customers. Innovation has long been the mantra for many successful companies. You have probably heard the term, "innovate or die." This term is primarily true because the fast pace most industries are taking to adopt new technologies is greater today than it was a decade ago. Think about how many companies are online and how many of these companies offer a quick and easy way to purchase their products or service. They provide free delivery, custom one-off products, incredible follow-up customer service, memberships, club discounts, etc. These are all important areas to consider when building your brand and determining how it may affect your ultimate customer experience.

The Customer Journey Analysis—A Simple Exercise

There are many exercises you can use to identify your customer experience and the journey they take from the first touchpoint to the experience of our product or service and after. We use a straightforward exercise called The Customer Journey analysis. Your customer's experience is at the core of how they will react to every touchpoint. Recently, we worked with a new client to help them with a rebrand. The information gained from The Customer Journey exercise was invaluable. Sometimes we identified minor issues and other times larger issues within the customer journey. For example, we discovered missing gaps in their email campaign as the call-to-action was not clear; therefore, many potential customers did not know what to do once they landed on their website. The solution was to create a customized and relatable landing page for every persona that spoke directly to them and also offered a clear "next step." This simple solution, among many others uncovered through The Customer Journey exercise, helped streamline the journey and create a positive experience.

The customer experience is one of the most overlooked aspects of branding and is also one of the most important. The Customer Journey Analysis is one of several exercises we use to identify opportunities and solve any issues.

This Is How To Do It:
1. Identify various customer personas.
2. With each persona, map out every touchpoint and step your customer takes. The details in your document should start from the very first time they encounter a touchpoint (advertisement, a referral, an email, etc.) to the use of your product or service and after.
3. Once you have created a detailed customer

Customer Experience (Journey)

journey, review all of the touchpoints and steps against your vision of a perfect customer experience. This is an excellent opportunity to remove or add all aspects of your customer journey and modify them to work with your brand vision.

In addition to using the The Customer Journey exercise, consider a location where you can share your product or service so people can try it. They can be your friends, neighbors, co-workers, or all of the above. Observe their behavior, understand how they connect with your brand and make detailed notes about their response to using your product or service. You will then be able to identify areas that still need attention, as well as areas that are exemplified as positive experiences.

Also, prior to this exercise, create a list of potential questions you would like answered to further understand your customer's needs and wants. In my experience, the best way to approach this is to ask open-ended questions that do not lead subjects to a specific answer. For instance, you may ask "What are the three top things you like about this product?" And, "What are the three least desirable attributes about this product?" Also, "How do you feel when you use this product?" This information will become very relevant when you are defining your brand message in the form of general communications and advertising.

Furthermore, you will uncover opportunities and roadblocks your customer might experience and be able to make any necessary corrections. Once you map out the complete buyer's journey, you should develop sales training, sales material, and marketing-related materials around all the key touchpoints.

Finally, through this exercise, understanding the sales objections will help you create or adjust your marketing and sales materials to ultimately assist you with overcoming the potential roadblocks within the sales process.

TIP: Make sure to document all comments and plan to use some of the feedback for testimonials within your future marketing strategy.

Consistency

There are many brands that have embraced and executed a sound brand consistency strategy. Take, for example, Apple. When I see a commercial, print ad, packaging, etc., I instantly know it is from Apple. Their approach to brand consistency is important to them because they understand the overall value of keeping the brand consistent. In my experience, brands that embrace brand consistency typically do much better than those that don't.

Why is consistency so important?
- Consistency increases brand equity
- Consistency creates trust and dependability
- Consistency creates recognition
- Consistency helps you display a level of professionalism
- Consistency eliminates brand confusion
- Consistency builds upon other marketing communications
- Consistency brings a unified message to your customers
- Consistency helps to convert prospects into buyers

Expectations are always aligned with consistency, and that is what drives trust—or the lack thereof. If you are consistent with your brand, you will gain the trust of your customers. And this trust, in turn, will give you a lifelong relationship. The relationship we have with brands is not much different from the relationships we have with our friends. It is essential to nurture the brand's character and uniqueness with consistent customer experiences. These experiences start with the very first touchpoint and goes all the way through to the purchase and post-purchase. Without consistency, you have chaos and distrust.

Perception vs. Emotional vs. Rational

Let's talk about how your customer makes a buying decision. It has long been known that people primarily make an emotional decision when purchasing a product or service. Our emotions are powerful and sometimes we are willing to sacrifice our rational thoughts to satisfy our emotional needs. Our emotional needs are usually tied to the pleasure or to the perceived satisfaction we get from using a product or service.

If the brand is perceived as more pleasurable than the nearest competitor, we are typically willing to pay more. The cycle involves getting emotionally engaged with a brand. We then consider the purchase which finally triggers our rational response.

For example, your friend comes to your house and shows off his new BMW. After a quick drive, you fall in love with the performance and how it makes you feel. At this point, you are emotionally engaged. Later that day, you decide to go online and check the availability of your favorite new car. Your passion for a new BMW comes first, then the rational side comes into play as you uncover new information like price or availability. Can you afford it? Will it fit in your garage? What will your significant other say about such a purchase? These rational thoughts are normal, albeit the initial passion "illusion" you had about your new car was more powerful than the facts. The illusion or perception we have about a brand can play an essential role in your customer's buying decision.

TIP: In planning your customer experience, take into consideration how your brand will be perceived across all touchpoints. What type of emotional bond will you have with your customer? What rational roadblock will keep your potential customer from choosing your brand?

A Meaningful Customer Engagement

By deeply understanding customers and identifying their needs, wants, and expectations, it's possible to put an action plan into place for your brand experience that aligns with your brand promise, culture, and vision. In turn, you will have loyal customers who are fully engaged and will recommend your brand to their friends.

CHAPTER SIX

Marketing and Sales

Whether you know it or not, your company articulates a brand promise with its name, logo, communications, and reputation. The key is to define the brand message and promise, and test their truth. If there is any flaw in the communication of your brand message and promise, you have to investigate, discover, and refine them to assert your true brand message and promise.

Marketing that lacks uniformity or truth befuddles the messaging and confuses consumers. The result is frustration on all fronts—business development slows, customers slink away, and marketing becomes a chore.

A simple, concise and true message must be woven throughout all communications. Every audience member should see, hear, and feel a consistent brand promise time after time.

First, you have to uncover your company's gospel truth. That involves revealing the brand elements discussed in earlier chapters such as the brand promise, brand essence, value proposition, positioning, etc. The cold, hard fact is that defining and conveying your brand's promise can be agonizing and daunting. The questions are tough. Telling the truth is even tougher—but the results are phenomenal and lasting. Tell the naked truth and you get:

- Improved efficiency and effectiveness in all marketing endeavors
- Higher market share and sharper competitive advantage
- Increased customer loyalty and revenues

The brand messages must be convincing, clear, and true to prompt your potential clients to act. Alternatively, many companies market their brand by simply sending out arbitrary messages. Ultimately, your brand message will be confusing and misguided.

Without the brand intelligence built into the broader

strategy, the message gets lost in the galaxy of media confusion. The message has no true destination. Meanwhile, any attempt to additional messages would ultimately compound the issue since there is no structure for how the subsequent message should complement the first.

It's clear you would never build a marketing strategy without researching where you are headed, who you want to reach, and how to best connect with them. Why tackle a marketing campaign without a strategic plan? Research can help your company definitively answer the questions below and articulate every message sent to your target audience:

- Do your potential clients know who you are?
- Do they know what you sell?
- Can they tell you apart from your competition?
- Can they readily perceive and count on your brand promise and value proposition?

Indeed, research can be grueling and even painful. However, the outcome of your hard work will simplify all other marketing endeavors.

Rather than haphazardly building or reworking your marketing campaign, execute an overall marketing plan that is destined to work. You can always count on research to provide guidance and get the job done right.

Marketing and Sales

In this chapter, we will explain the details that will help you build a strong marketing and sales foundation.

We will cover these topics.
- Understanding the Buyer
- Who Are Your Competitors
- Market Analysis
- Market Size
- Market Segments
- Channels and Distribution
- Budgeting
- Marketing Tactics
- And lastly, the Wrap Up

Branding your new product or service started with the discovery phase and then moved into uncovering your brand message and story. These were all achieved through the discovery of multiple brand elements such as your brand essence, brand character, value proposition, etc.

The marketing and sales strategy for your new business launch should be well thought-out to enable both a great new brand and a successful launch.

Finally, the following sections will build upon the information you were able to gather and create within the

Brand Building chapter. As you build your brand and prepare to launch it, you will find yourself moving back and forth between these areas until you are perfectly happy with the overall direction. This will require some patience.

6.1 Your Customer

We touched on the customer journey earlier. The information gained from that exercise should be integrated into this phase. Understanding your customers and getting feedback from them early and often will provide you with an arsenal of data you can use to improve your brand.

Furthermore, below are additional questions you should answer to help understand your customer better.

- Who are the people buying your products and services?
- Why would they purchase your product or service?
- What does your customer need or want?
- What are their expectations?

Based on your brand vision, it may be helpful to describe your ideal customer.

We recommend building a customer profile and identifying your best customer characteristics. Begin by writing out each type of customer you will be selling to. This is commonly known as personas.

A buyer persona is a thorough description of your ideal customer that captures their needs, challenges, aspirations, beliefs, values, biases, and concerns addressed by your products or services.

We often use The Customer Journey analysis in the previous chapter to help us gather pertinent information about customer personas. This is a great exercise to help understand the steps each of your buyer personas takes to make a purchase and use your product. The analysis is basically a short story from the very beginning: when a customer first connects to your brand all the way through the customer's purchase and the use of your product or service. Also, there are plenty of research firms, in addition to your own research, which will help you better understand your potential customers. Identifying who they are and how you can fulfill their needs and wants are key.

The following list includes some great ideas to help uncover who your customers really are:

- Open a dialogue by calling potential customers and asking them several quick questions.
- If you have an actual face-to-face interaction with your customer, simply ask.
- Integrate a feedback or survey form.

- Hire a research company to collect data about your customer's demographics, lifestyles, buying habits, etc.
- Gather insight from your sales team.
- Go out and be seen where your customers spend their time.
- Use social media to gather information.
- Create an event where you can engage with your current and prospective customers.

6.2 Competitors

After you have a better understanding of your potential customers, the next phase is to understand your competitors. During the branding portion of the discovery phase, you dove into your competitors' brands. Use the information collected and apply it to this section.

Here is a quick list of what to look for:

Again, you may have uncovered some of this in the branding section. It is important to review and look at this data through the marketing and sales lens.

- Background info
- Number of employees
- Review of products and services

Marketing and Sales

- Client list
- Revenue and pricing
- Social media presence
- Online marketing techniques
- News and press releases
- A detailed list of your competitor's services vs. your services

At this point, you have collected an enormous amount of information. This information will be key as you start to uncover more about your market.

Regarding competitors, review the data in detail and pay special attention to how they strategically market and sell. And gather as much information as possible on your competitors brand message, brand promise, differentiators, etc. Ultimately, you should have an excellent understanding of what differentiates your new business brand from your competitors.

As we already know, visual communication is very important for your brand. Your competitors will make all of their marketing tactics readily available for you. In addition to the research mentioned earlier in this section, take into consideration the visual brand of each competitor. Gather their marketing materials and compare them to yours.

6.3 Market Analysis

An essential part of the marketing and sales plan is the market analysis. Conducting a thorough market analysis will help you reduce the risk of your investment. In the following sections we will review market size, market trends, and segmentation. The information and sources you need vary with each business.

This goes without saying: If you are also involved in a rebrand initiative, a thorough marketing analysis is an essential part of your business intelligence.

Look at industry-specific resources. Keep in mind, it is a completely different process selling a child's toy versus selling a medical device. For any new brand, there are plenty of publicly available data sources such as your local chamber, Department of Commerce, Department of Labor, US Census Bureau, www.business.gov, and www.usa.gov/business. You should find a great deal of key information that will lead you to the right resources.

6.4 Market Size

Defining the market size can be a little confusing. There are several ways to get an idea of how big the market is within your industry. This is important to understand because it will also help you learn how to market your brand.

Marketing and Sales

Several key questions to answer are:

- How many potential buyers are in your market?
- How big is the industry in relation to overall current sales? How big is the market for your specific product or service?
- What is the total potential size of your market and your potential growth? Let's use the smartphone market as an example. As of today, it is starting to flatten out. With in-depth research you might find that there may still may be a niche market. Smartphone companies will continue to explore expansions into global markets to continue their growth. There may be plenty of potential buyers in each global market. A detailed 3 to 5-year forecast might provide some clues.
- Do you see the market growing or shrinking?
- Lastly, consider market trends. Whether you are selling consumer products or B2B products, you need to be aware of trends. How are buyers responding to trends, such as environmental trends or political trends? Is there a possible trend where your product fills your potential customer's needs? You may have already uncovered this information earlier during your SWOT analysis.

6.5 Market Segments

Defining your market segments will help you concentrate your marketing dollars within a segment of your total audience. It's all about efficiency.

Marketing strategies, tactics, and campaigns can be tailored to meet the needs of each market segment. This will bring a new sense of engagement with your new customers. They will feel and believe you are directly addressing their specific needs and wants.

To get started, divide your market into segments that target the different individual needs of your buyers. Remember the work you completed earlier to define various personas? These personas should be considered as part of your market segment.

Depending on your unique brand model, you should explore different market segment types to expand your potential market size.

These are the most common segments.
- Demographic
- Geographic
- Behavioral
- Lifestyles
- Usage Patterns

- Persona
- Income
- And more...

Segmentation can be complicated and it can be easy to make mistakes. Common mistakes are: creating too many segments, defining a slice of a segment that is too small, not identifying trends across segments, creating a broad segment that should be segmented, and not identifying segments to match media distribution.

Once you have defined various market segments, fine-tune your message for each segment. Use the information to provide different offers, fine-tune your pricing, adjust your sales tactics, create unique advertising campaigns, and modify your marketing messages so they are relevant to your prospective customers.

6.6 Channels and Distribution

The channel and distribution model you put into place will greatly affect your brand perception. Whether you have a product or a service, you need to define how your product or service will be distributed and what channels to use.

Every step of your customer's experience has a significant influence on your brand perception. Moreover, there is a cautionary tale here. You may have created the best brand message and story, and also created the best product or service, but your customers may get aggravated if your product or service is difficult to acquire. This is a direct reflection of your brand. Depending on your product or service, think of the most practical and cost-effective way to distribute it and also consider what will be the best experience for your customer.

Remember the company MoviePass? When they launched their $10 a month subscription service for unlimited movies, their subscription rate grew from roughly 20,000 to more than 600,000 members in less than four months. This was a monumental success for them. But unfortunately, many new members did not get their cards in a reasonable amount of time and MoviePass customer service was overwhelmed with requests. This caused many problems with their brand perception, trust, brand equity, and resulted in the loss of many current and potentially new customers. It generally takes time for companies to recover from such a major snafu. All of this could have been prevented with foresight and a sound distribution plan.

As you decide your distribution plan for your product or service, think about what kind of experience you want

Marketing and Sales

your customers to have. If you have a consumer product, will your customers get your product at Walmart or Nordstrom? Or will they purchase it online from Amazon? Each scenario creates a unique customer experience.

Again, using Apple as an example, they found it difficult to provide their products through retailers such as Target and Best Buy. They learned many employees of these retailers were not well versed in Apple's products, therefore, ultimately hurting the brand experience with their prospective customers. Strategically, they decided it was best to develop their own retail stores where every employee was trained on the capabilities and benefits of their products. This was a brilliant move because Apple could manage the customer experience and also engage with their customers to better understand their needs.

There are a lot of marketing situations to consider if your brand is a service. Are you providing a service to customers such as carpet cleaning or a service where people come to your place of business, like an oil change? Is it an online service?

All of these scenarios create a unique opportunity to establish a strong bond with your customers. Understanding the various caveats with distribution will also help you make any necessary corrections in advance for a better brand experience for your customer.

TIP: Remember, the brand experience from the very first touchpoint with a product or service plays a big part in your brand perception.

6.7 Budget

It's time to have that "Budget" discussion. We aren't going to spend time on financial statements and projections. However, we will discuss allocations in regard to marketing and sales budgets.

It's important to allocate the appropriate budget to accomplish the goals and priorities you have identified. Let's look at this in percentages. If you want to grow 25%, but only invest pennies, you will be disappointed.

Let's review at three budget options:

First - The "Maintenance" Budget: Allocating 2-3% of your estimated revenue to support branding and marketing activities. This level of budget could support current customers with simple marketing and sales tools. The return on investment will likely not be ambitious growth.

Second - The "Attention" Budget: Consider a marketing budget of 4-5% of projected revenue. This is to attract new prospects and retain current customers. Consider this budget for roughly a 10% growth goal.

Marketing and Sales

Third, we have the "Let's-Grow-Baby-Grow" Budget: Take a look at allocating 6% or more of your revenue. This is for accelerating growth and results. Your focus is on driving leads, conversions, and sales. A goal might be to increase market share and kick your competitors to the curb. This budget should consider an initial growth goal of 20%.

These budgets should also be integrated with measurable metrics. The data collected will provide useful information for return on investment (ROI) ratios. Furthermore, this information can be used to modify expenses in marketing strategies, tactics, and campaigns.

So, be sure to budget appropriately in your first year. One of the most significant failures we see is the inability to take advantage of a grand brand launch due to a lack of sufficient funds. Essentially, do you want to start your new business slowly or give it a strong push from the very beginning? We'll cover this more in-depth in the Launch chapter.

TIP: It is essential to set expectations realistically and adequately when you launch a new brand. Part of this is understanding the budget required to really grow a business. The first year of any new brand launch will be a much more significant investment. This is because the effort in building your new brand from scratch will require you to invest in help from accountants, attorneys, branding experts, and designers. You should have a healthy budget set aside for optimal growth.

6.8 Marketing Tactics

One of my first and probably the best lesson I learned was not in a classroom or working with a Fortune 500 company. I learned it from an old Italian shop owner. When I was a young kid living in Iowa, my friends and I used to frequent an old Italian grocery store near my Junior High School. They made the best Italian sandwiches in the state! One day as I was leaving the store I noticed a big barrel of apples with a sign that read "25 cents each." I visited the store after school several days in a row and noticed the barrel was still pretty full. A few more days had passed. When I visited the store again, as I was getting ready to check out, to my surprise I noticed most of the apples in the barrel were gone. "Where did all the apples go?" I asked the store owner. With a big grin he pointed to the new sign that read "Three apples for $1." He proceeded to tell me his customers love deals, so he gave them "a deal" they could not resist. His aptitude to understand his customers and make the necessary change in his marketing tactic was, in my opinion, brilliant.

Marketing and Sales

At this point, you should inherently understand your brand, including all of the elements, and apply it to a strong marketing tactic. The information you have gathered about your brand, your personas, your competitors, and your market data will be helpful in this phase of the brand launch.

Additionally, you should outline the best tactics to reach your unique customers. Below is a list of potential, marketing ideas to consider. If you understand your customers as described in earlier chapters and sections, narrowing down some of the ideas below should be much easier. Remember, at first, identifying and executing successful marketing tactics can be a little trial and error.

The following list may provide some ideas to reflect upon.

Evangelism Marketing

This is a form of advanced word-of-mouth marketing. Companies recruit customers as advocates to help spread the word about their brand.

Proximity Marketing

Using smartphones and other devices, companies can send localized wireless communications in the form of advertising to the customer's smartphone and other devices that have Bluetooth, WiFi, and NFC capabilities.

Mass Marketing

This is traditional marketing geared to the masses. Companies ignore market segments and broadcast their advertising to reach the largest amount of people possible.

Mobile Marketing:

Since many customers use mobile devices, mobile marketing is a great way to reach them. Taking advantage of today's technology, advertising to a mobile device can be accomplished through QR codes, SMS text messaging, MMS multimedia messaging, and mobile-friendly websites to name a few.

Transactional Marketing

Let's make some sales! The main objective of transactional marketing is to make as many sales as possible in the shortest amount of time. A good example is QVC—they offer a time-based promotion strategy strictly designed to make the sale.

Relationship Marketing

Establishing a relationship with your customers is a great way to build brand loyalty. The main goal of relationship marketing is to nurture the relationship and understand the needs of your customer.

Scarcity Marketing

Only 5 left! This technique uses the principle that there are only a few who can afford a product or service, there are limited quantities, or there are only a number of seats left for an event.

Word-of-Mouth Marketing (WOM)

Engage your customers and give them a reason to talk about your brand—in a good way. Satisfied customers will inevitably brag about your unique brand. And there are many ways to create that unique brand experience with your customers. Examples such as that amazing concert you just attended, Apple's all glass see-through store in NY, fish tossing at Seattle's historic Pike Place Market, etc.

Content Marketing

The main focus of content marketing is to provide the potential consumer with relevant and valuable information to persuade them to purchase your product or service.

Thought Leadership

Are you an authority in your field? Then thought leadership is for you. Use your expertise and share it with your customers to build trust and engagement with your brand.

Make My Brand Bigger

Diversity Marketing

This is sometimes referred to "in-culture" marketing. Through thoughtful research, diversity marketing can help many companies expand their market share while at the same time make a concerted effort to connect different people with different backgrounds.

Public Relations (PR) Marketing

Building a strong reputation should not solely lie on marketing and communications. Public relations is a great way to create positive media coverage and head off negative assumptions about your brand.

Online and Offline

Take into consideration your overall marketing strategy and make sure everything is in line with your brand message. Sometimes this can be a little tricky because many people inherently create confusion with their communication between their online strategy and their offline strategy.

Social Media Marketing

Not every business needs to use social media marketing. But if you do, there are many options for social media including platforms such as Facebook, LinkedIn, Twitter, Instagram, etc. Many of these are cost effective and should be considered, especially if your customers are engaged and using them. Otherwise, it is best to look at other options to reach and engage with your customers.

Alliance Marketing

Also known as "co-op" marketing. This strategy aligns two or more companies with the purpose of sharing resources to market and reach customers. These companies typically have the same goals.

B2B and B2C Marketing

These indicate two different forms of business transactions, business-to-business and business-to-consumer. The main difference between the two marketing strategies are the focus on how the company uses their marketing dollar. Ultimately, I like to refer to our strategy as B2P, business-to-people. Although there are distinct differences between the B2B and B2C strategies, it is my belief we are always speaking and marketing directly to "people."

Seasonal Marketing

Fourth of July, Memorial Day, and Back-to-School are several examples of great seasonal events your company can leverage through targeted campaigns.

Make My Brand Bigger

Promotional Marketing

Retail and service brands can use promotional marketing to entice customers. The main purpose is to persuade your customer to take immediate action with 40%-off sales, BOGO offers, limited-time offers, etc.

Coupons

Clipping coupons is considered a chore, but there are a lot of people who find pleasure in saving money. Coupons can be either tangible or are offered instantly online.

Guerrilla Marketing

This is an unconventional way to reach your customers without spending a lot of money. Strategically, guerrilla marketing suggests that you use your time, knowledge, and imagination to reach your customers.

SEO and SEM

To be relevant today, you need a website. You have to be found online. But building and creating a website is not enough. The main goal of Search Engine Optimization is to optimize your website through various techniques such as incorporating unique keywords, creating content-specific blogs, backlinks, and social sharing to ensure your website appears high on the search engine list. Search Engine Marketing (SEM) involves the use of paid advertising. Many companies such as Google, Facebook, and Instagram offer solutions for paid advertising.

Email and Drip Marketing

Email marketing is one of the best ways to reach customers who have already provided you with their basic personal information. Email marketing, in conjunction with drip marketing, is a great way to "drip" relevant information to your customers and not overwhelm them with too much at once.

Event Marketing

One of the best ways to engage your customers is event marketing. Whether you market at a trade show, music festival, or special dinner, your connection with your customers will be personal and engaging.

Outbound and Inbound

The premise behind outbound marketing is that you push your brand message out using tactics such as trade shows, cold calling, email blasts, etc. Inbound marketing subscribes to the idea that your customers found you through useful content such as blogs, carefully optimized websites (SEO), and social media engagement.

Direct Marketing

Communicate directly to your customer with catalog distribution methods, direct mail, flyers, etc. With direct marketing, it is crucial to set up a system to track how well your marketing efforts are performing.

Freebie Marketing

People love free stuff! Getting people to try your product or service is typically the biggest challenge. This strategy's main purpose is to lower the risk threshold for the customer and entice them to give your product or service a try.

Each previously mentioned tactics and strategy should be directly correlate to the customers you want to reach based on the brand research you have collected throughout the discovery section.

A key takeaway: Understand where your buyers look for information and be relevant.

6.9 Wrap Up

We covered a significant amount of material to give you the foundation for a solid Marketing and Sales Strategy to launch your brand.

Marketing and Sales

Here are the main key takeaways:

- Your customers are the lifeblood of your company.
- Map out the complete buyer's journey using the The Customer Journey analysis. Understanding sales objections can help you create effective marketing and sales material.
- Know your competitors better than they know themselves. Get as much information as you can about how your competitors are marketing and selling their products and services.
- Market Analysis. Once again, identify segments that target the different specific needs of your buyers. Remember with Channels and Distribution, the brand experience from the very first touchpoint plays a big part in your brand experience.
- Concerning the budget. Set expectations properly when you launch a new brand. Understand the budget required to really grow your business. The first year of any new brand launch will be a much bigger investment.

CHAPTER SEVEN

Visual Communications

As an instructor at Metropolitan State University in Denver, I taught several classes including Advanced Visual Communications. One of the best pieces of advice I gave my students was, "A picture is worth a thousand words; just be sure they are the correct words." This is a profound statement, which speaks to the basic principle of developing a sound visual communication strategy. Everything should be considered. Including all of the hard work you put into building your brand in the previous chapters, defining a strong marketing strategy and every visual communication element such as images, colors, icons, photography, fonts, company and product logos, and brochure design.

Visual Communications

From a behavioral science point of view, we are bombarded with marketing messages every second of our waking lives. The ability for people to filter this information is impressive to say the least. We process and absorb images in milliseconds, which is much faster than reading text.

Moreover, the importance of creating unique and memorable visuals that support your brand are monumental to the success of your brand.

There are many benefits of creating a sound visual communication strategy. They are a clearer communication with your customers, an improved brand consistency, strong brand loyalty, trust, the ability for you to communicate a complex idea in a simple way that your customer can understand, and improved efficiency in your various communication materials.

Visual Communication plays a key role in the launch of your brand. There are four upcoming sections.

- Logos and Colors
- Brand Identity
- Brand Standards
- The Wrap Up

7.1 Logos and Colors

Although exciting, designing a logo can be an exhausting process. The process will engage both your creative and analytical skills. I highly recommend hiring a branding firm for this stage of the visual brand development. The skills necessary to successfully execute a well-designed logo typically take years to develop.

If you plan on tackling this on your own, following the phased approach listed below will keep you focused and should help you complete the tasks for a logo design. Seasoned design professionals around the world use these techniques. To prepare for this exercise, it is vital to have a basic understanding of design principles and design software such as Adobe Illustrator or a comparable design software program.

You should also remember these primary fundamental objectives for a successful logo design: the logo must be unique, it must be memorable, it must instill an essence of the brand, and it must convey a visual element that is unique to your brand.

As an example, take a look at several logos for companies that are very successful. The Apple and Nike logo designs are simple, yet distinct. Coca-Cola's logo has a flowing typeface that instills a unique feeling. And John Deere's

Visual Communications

primary green color along with their iconic jumping deer are designed to create a connection with farmers.

Initial Fact Gathering: Collect a summary of information from the work and exercises done previously about your brand. As a starting point, you will need to identify the name of your company and how the name will be used within the logo. The brand name should be unique to the industry. Also, consider all aspects of your brand such as the position of the brand, a brief description of the company, who the audience is, a visual collection of competitor logos and descriptions, and most importantly what key messages the brand wants to convey. Once you have created a clear summary of the company information, you can then proceed with the creation of a visual brand board.

Execute the Visual Brand Board: A visual brand board is an initial design board of collages or collections of found images depicting possible corporate color palettes, stylized photography, various fonts, and any other proposed visual styles and visual languages. The visual brand board will serve as the initial starting point for collaboration between you and all the stakeholders. After you receive feedback from the team on the individual elements represented on the visual brand board, and you are comfortable with the feedback, an updated brand board may be required. The final brand board will provide you with an enormous amount of visual inspiration to initiate the logo development.

Initial Logo Brainstorming: Brainstorm and sketch ideas acquired from the initial fact-gathering phase and from the brand board development. These sketches are merely ideas on paper. You should sketch initial quick ideas (thumbnails), anywhere from several dozens to a hundred or more. The purpose of this particular exercise is to accumulate as many quick visual ideas as possible.

Once you have completed a series of ideas, circle the ideas you believe have the potential visual characteristics. This is called a short list. This short list of ideas is further refined by a series of more detailed sketches and font explorations. These font explorations are an accumulation of various font families using the company's name. The combination of your sketches and various fonts will provide you with a small set of ideas to further develop with the assistance of a design application such as Adobe Illustrator.

TIP: Less is more. A well-designed logo is typically simple (without complexity). In most cases, the more you add to the logo the worse it gets. The purpose of a logo is to act as a reminder of the brand, much like an icon.

Final Logo Development: As a result of the initial logo brainstorming phase, it is usual to have identified ten to fif-

Visual Communications

teen logo design directions. Next, scan your ideas, import them into your design application, and refine your designs to your desired outcome. These design directions should be rendered in black and white, with a short list rendered in color. These are to be reviewed, tested and further refined down to a maximum of three concepts for presentation to stakeholders. Additional refinements can be performed after the initial presentation as needed. The approved logo, which may include a symbol and typography, will be applied to key external communication items identified by priority. These items may include, but are not limited to, business cards, letterheads, envelopes, web banner ads, trade show booths, etc.

This book, *Make My Brand Bigger,* should help you create a big and successful brand that resonates through every touchpoint with your customers **without** the need to place the logo as big as possible everywhere you can.

As I mentioned earlier, I recommend hiring the right brand agency to develop your logo. Logo development is a craft and these professionals will create a logo that is not only unique to your brand, but also has the expertise and knowledge behind it. Your new logo is a representation of your brand. Its purpose is to remind people what the brand stands for and provide a consistent representation of your brand. In addition to developing a strong logo, you should consider your company colors. The corporate primary colors are typically derived from your logo but can also contain supporting colors to use as accents.

TIP: With the help of your attorney, you should be able to identify if your logo is protectable as artistic work.

7.2 Brand Identity

Defining your company's brand through a great logo is not enough. A well-designed logo should be incorporated into various marketing and sales communications. Once you have chosen your logo, you will need to put it to the test.

As you did in the Final Logo Development section, place the logo on several mock-ups such as a business card, letterhead, website homepage, brochure, trade show exhibit, and so on.

This is where we begin to build the identity of the brand. Basically, this is how the brand will look in various mediums and how the brand will translate its brand story throughout each piece. A well-designed brand identity will evolve over time. As you encounter new information about your brand, it is smart to review your visual brand and make any necessary adjustments. Obviously, we are talking about minor modifications to the overall brand except for the logo. Your logo should be left alone and you should push back on suggestions to change or modify it.

Building a strong brand identity is crucial. If done correctly, it will alleviate confusion and eliminate misguided brand messages that could otherwise cost you a great deal of time and money.

TIP: Whether you're doing this on your own or are working with a branding agency, print out each piece. Don't rely on viewing your identity items solely on your computer screen. When you print these items, you can clearly review each piece and gain perspective on the various dimensions such as size, proportions, white space, legibility, etc.

7.3 Brand Standards

You have created a multitude of marketing pieces. Now your goal is to create consistency across all of your mediums. Your new brand needs standards and guidelines that are easily accessible to all internal and external parties authorized to develop the brand. The Brand Standards will guide anyone who is charged with building your brand and maintaining your brand consistency.

It has been my experience that a well-developed "brand standards guide" should be flexible enough to encourage creativity, while at the same time be consistent with the brand message.

Your brand standards should be developed to meet your needs. As an example, we have developed brand standards that were several hundred pages in length covering not only the company standards but also multiple products. They can be daunting to create, but well worth it when you have multiple departments and people in various locations executing your brand message and consistency. Moreover, even if you do not have multiple departments or various people in various locations, creating a strong brand standards guide will help keep you on brand message and provide useful information. It will also help communicate an already well-crafted brand message. This, don't forget, helps to create consistency, build brand loyalty and trust with your customers.

The following list are example topics to include in your brand standards:

- Company and product naming standards
- Company and product boilerplates
- Legal descriptions which have been previously vetted by your attorney
- Benefit descriptions
- Keywords to reinforce your brand message

Visual Communications

- Brand message talking points to help your copywriters and sales staff
- A defined tone for your company
- Also include visual brand examples, such as:
    - Logo and color standards
    - Font standards
    - Photography style standards
    - Graphic standards
    - Icon standards
    - Brochure examples
    - Advertising examples
    - Banner ad examples
    - And so on!

TIP: The use of your newly developed brand standards guide will help to facilitate familiarity with customers through a consistent message. Consistency is an essential key to building a memorable brand.

7.4 Wrap Up!

We've covered many great insights to help you build a strong foundation for your visual communications.

Let's review some of the highlights again.

- Your new logo is a representation of your brand.
- While you are building your brand identity, place the logo on several mock-ups such as a business card, brochure, and website. Then make any necessary changes to conform to an overall visual brand.
- Brand standards help businesses save money and time—and assist with building brand consistency. They also help you stay on message throughout various marketing materials and sales tactics.

CHAPTER EIGHT

Pre-Launch and Launch Planning

***WOW!** Let's get your brand ready for launch!*

You have completed the discovery phase and filled in all of the gaps. You should have already completed the branding portion to include specific details about your brand message, brand story, and visual communications.

In addition, you have mapped out a strong marketing and sales strategy. The launch of your new brand is an opportunity you should not take lightly. This is your time to seize the day.

Each launch phase is essential. We will cover them

in detail. The three launch phases you should consider in your planning are:
- Pre-Launch
- Launch
- Post-Launch

Pre-launch planning will help you avoid catastrophic issues. There are many reasons companies fail—from the timing of the launch relative to trends or the economy, to not having the right financial resources needed to reach your target audience.

Quick note: Don't take the launch of your brand lightly. If done properly, you should get a lot of buzz in the marketplace to help catapult your business with new customers and new leads. Also, plan accordingly. A successful launch will generate sales with new customers. Therefore, you want to make sure you take care of your customers from the very beginning and leave them with a positive first impression.

8.1 Let's Get Organized
Goals and Objectives:

To begin, I recommend you create an outline of your expectations. These should be summarized in your overall

Pre-Launch and Launch Planning

goals. For example, one of your goals for the launch might be to gain 500 new customers in the first week. Or your goal might be to get coverage from the top three news networks. These are great; however, first you should detail your goals with actionable objectives and tactics. Everything you do with the launch should be measurable.

For example, last summer we worked with a national insurance company to launch a new application that helps their customers record and note insurance related accidents. We defined a series of goals and objectives for each phase of the launch and post-launch. We set up three phases: pre-launch, launch, and post-launch. These included time-based goals and objectives and required a detailed set of rules to document measurable metrics such as website clickthroughs, application downloads, customer usage time, and more. Using these simple metrics, we established goals for each phase and customized the marketing strategy and tactics to fit the desired outcome. While we were greatly successful in meeting all of the goals and objectives, we also gained beneficial insight into their customer's needs, wants, and behaviors.

After you finalize the outline of your goals and objectives, apply the SMART Goal system to all of your goals to help verify your direction.

The SMART Goal system:

- **Specific:** Make sure you have a specific goal vs. a goal that is vague.
- **Measurable:** All goals should have something that can be measured.
- **Actionable**: What are the tasks required to reach the goal?
- **Realistic:** Make sure goals can be obtained during post-launch measurable metrics.
- **Time-bound:** Assign a date to each goal and objectives. It will help you review how you're doing.

First begin writing each of these in draft form to get a general view of what your launch might look like. After you have completed the draft, refine your SMART Goal strategy to meet your goals and objectives. Basically, define your goals and objectives with measurable numbers.

You can also use this information to help communicate your goals and objectives with other parties responsible for helping with your brand and additionally communicate your expectations. Clearly defined objectives will help you understand how to spend your launch budget. Also, use this information to review goals, refine objectives, and make tactical changes.

Pre-Launch and Launch Planning

Launch Timeline

The launch timeline should include all necessary players and resources. This should be as detailed as possible. My recommendation is to pick a launch day and a launch week. This will allow you to plan all activities around the Big Event. The timeline should take into consideration all of your resources, individual responsibilities and, of course, the budget.

Don't forget, this launch is a celebration of your new brand. Early planning, as well as laying out the responsibilities and resources before the launch, will help you alleviate any major hang-ups at launch time. The timeline should take into consideration all resources, individual responsibilities, and the budget.

Launch Team

Having the right people on your launch team is paramount to the initial success of your brand. Carefully choosing the right people for the right task will ease your stress.

Part of your strategy might be to choose a Launch Leader who is devoted to your launch success. Select outside resources carefully. These are partners such as PR firms, marketing agencies, and branding firms. These should be people you enjoy working with, people you trust, and people that have a great amount of expertise.

Public Relations

Public Relations (PR) plays an important role in any launch. When you develop your brand, you should have defined your brand story, what makes your brand unique, and why anyone should use your product or service over your competitors. This is the story you will push with PR. Get your PR strategy ready well before the launch and integrate it into your launch plan.

If you work with a Public Relations firm, which I highly recommend, consider creating a media kit that is both printed and available on your website. When you lay out your launch timeline, remember to take advantage of the most opportune time to pitch your brand story.

TIP: You don't have to wait until the actual launch date. You can tease your brand story early and often, even before the launch.

Branding Agency

Hiring a good branding agency will make all the difference. They will be responsible for helping you develop a strong brand and define your brand story. A good branding agency should not only create a compelling brand mes-

Pre-Launch and Launch Planning

sage, but also create a compelling visual language to support it. With their expertise, the branding agency will help drive the process and provide support where you need it. There are two essential parts of any strong brand. The contextual side which is the written and verbal message (your brand story), and the visual side which helps further reinforce that story.

The Budget

The launch budget is almost always forgotten or pushed under the rug. Bigger budgets fuel success. Many companies spend all of their budget getting the company ready for the launch. And many will completely neglect to budget for the actual launch of their brand. The single biggest obstacle to a successful launch is underfunding. So, let's dig into the process a little deeper.

Developing a budget spreadsheet for your launch enables you to look at the launch plan realistically. Every actionable item requires time and money. As noted before, most companies don't place enough emphasis on establishing the budget of a new brand launch.

Let's get into the steps of creating a budget:

1. First, review your launch goals and objectives.

2. Based on your goals and objectives, develop a detailed plan that is measurable.
3. Itemize and prioritize each deliverable.
4. Assign a cost to each element. This should also include staff time.
5. Review each deliverable for the likelihood of what will be successful based on your launch goals and objectives.
6. Finally, ask yourself, "Can we actually do this?" "Is it achievable?"

This might seem like a long process. But, once you have completed the budget spreadsheet, you'll rest a little easier knowing you have a strong plan in place with achievable goals and a realistic budget.

Furthermore, review our brief discussion on setting the three budget options mentioned in Chapter 6.

Your goals and objectives must match your budget.

8.2 Pre-Launch Implementation

We don't want to forget the activities that lead up to the launch date. Pre-launch success leads to launch success. The purpose of the pre-launch is to gather all of your

Pre-Launch and Launch Planning

key stakeholders together. This is a significant milestone to ensure you're on the right path.

Your pre-launch implementation involves several meetings with your launch team and includes double-checking all deliverables, uncovering any issues, and potentially sidelining any surprises.

It is essential to review all the components scheduled for launch day. Who is in charge of key strategies and tactics? Do you have the right contact list for all of your resources?

By reviewing your launch day details, you will be able to identify in advance the gaps that could be potentially embarrassing or problematic. And don't forget about all the technology you're planning to use during your launch day and week.

For example, if your launch requires your customers to go online and purchase your product, it is a good idea to confirm in advance that your shopping cart is working correctly, and also validate that you have enough Internet bandwidth. Remember the government healthcare fiasco where their site kept crashing? Or, for instance, let's say you are planning to launch your new business at a trade show. Have you tried to run the software demo on the video screen? Does it work remotely? These seemingly simple items can become major headaches and ruin your brand's reputation if you don't do a thorough test prior to the actual launch date.

8.3 Launch Implementation: Internal
Great branding starts <u>within</u> your company first.

Let's talk about the internal strategy. This might come as a surprise to some of you. Your employees are your most essential Brand Ambassadors. They need to be on board with the new brand. The comprehensive communications plan you develop should include elements to motivate and excite your employees.

How do we get employees on board? Pull together an internal team by soliciting help from various departments. They don't all have to be from the Marketing Team. Typically, the best team is a good cross-section of the company employees. Next, share the brand story with them and develop that exciting culture. Gather insight and collect ideas from the group. Not just about the brand, but also about the launch. Integrate and share your goals with them so they understand the expectations. Again, they are the best Brand Ambassadors for your new brand. Use them to help deliver your great brand story and assign various responsibilities for the launch. Let them take ownership.

Pre-Launch and Launch Planning

Building an internal team to help you launch your brand should be done prior to any external launch.

Remember, a great brand starts within your company first. Give your employees the tools they need in advance to be successful. Spend the necessary time in this area and you will be on the right track for a successful launch.

Get your employees excited

While planning the launch with the internal team, it is wise to consider all the employees of the company. Employee engagement should be done in advance of launching the new brand to the public. So, here are some ideas we have used with other brand launches: Design fun T-shirts and place them on every desk the day before the launch of your new brand. And speaking of swag, hire a local specialty products company to provide you with exceptional ideas based on your budget. These can include pencils, pens, mugs, hats, coasters, etc.

Other ideas for launch day might include bringing in an ice cream cart for all of your staff. Who doesn't like free ice cream, right? You could also create a fun "company video" featuring the new brand. Have a special day for employees to explore the new brand through storytelling, short seminars, etc.

Make your employee engagement a success. Your brand depends on it.

8.4 Launch Implementation: External

Timing is everything. With your already established launch timeline, utilizing the great internal team you have put together, refine the timeline for an external launch. At this point, you should have identified your launch day and launch week. Make sure it is on the calendar. Launch week is critical. Have a daily plan of what employee-facing activities are happening as well as potential external, customer-facing activities.

Whether you're a Fortune 500 company or a small entrepreneurial company with several employees, you can still take advantage of this launch strategy.

Below are some useful steps to get you started:

1. Create ownership by assigning a specific person to each task on the master list of deliverables.
2. Also, be sure to cross check the overall strategy against your external launch goals.
3. Finally, define and secure any outside partnerships you need to make this day and week a huge success.

Pre-Launch and Launch Planning

The external launch is where you will create the most impact and win. What comes to mind for external brand launch items? Think big! When you launch your new brand, it should be a huge event. It is the beginning of a great new product or service that will affect many people's lives.

I often hear the concern from many businesses who wonder how extravagant their brand launch should be. This is normal because people are used to the large-scale brand launch campaigns from companies with big budgets such as Coca-Cola, Apple, BMW, and so on. My word of advice is, "Don't worry about it." Focus on your brand and your customers. As I mentioned before, every business is different. Focus on what is important to get your message out to your audience.

As we discussed, a robust marketing strategy is key to your launch. There are plenty of ideas to help get your brand noticed. Do you want to reach local, national, or global prospects? How about a newsletter, initiated during launch week? Using techniques like this will help you capture email addresses as well. You might also consider direct mail such as a dimensional piece or postcards. Email campaigns are always relevant too. Think about social media campaigns utilizing Facebook, Twitter, Instagram, etc. All of these options should be considered.

8.5 Wrap Up!

Let's wrap this up with some key takeaways.

- Designate a launch leader. This person is the go-to for all activities and plans.
- Don't forget to hire the right outside experts, such as a PR agency, event coordinator and an expert branding agency.
- The budget. We have talked about money, money, money many times. Make sure you have allocated the proper budget to launch your new brand successfully.
- Here is a pre-launch tip that I really like. Take extra time to go through your launch day in fine detail. This will help you find any missteps in your launch plan.
- For the external launch... Think Big!!! When you launch your new brand, it should be a major event.

CHAPTER NINE

Post-Launch, Analysis, and Refinement

Let's keep the momentum going.

Often forgotten are the thank you cards, the vast amount of information gained during the launch, the follow-up with vendors. Here we will discuss how we can utilize everything and leverage additional opportunities to keep the momentum going.

In this chapter, we will cover details of the post-launch strategy. First, we will look at post-launch goals and objectives. Second, we will discuss ways to ramp-up your marketing and sales strategy. Then we will look at key points to review your brand message and story.

9.1 Post-Launch Goals and Objectives

Let's presume you had an exciting launch week. You have a new brand, and you did a great job spreading the word about your brand. Let's not forget your post-launch strategy. Planning a post-launch strategy will help you maintain the momentum and reveal opportunities for on-going marketing and sales.

Branding is an ongoing strategy with tactful executions, and it doesn't stop with the launch of your brand. The post-launch timeline can continue for quite a while. Stay on top of your new brand strategy. Keep it shiny and new, and adjust it as needed. We prefer activities that can be measured over time as you roll out your brand strategy. These metrics should not stop at the launch stage. With today's technology, it is easier than ever to set up a monthly activity report to share with your team.

You should already have in place a sound strategy with goals and objectives to keep the momentum going after the launch of your brand. These goals and objectives can be aligned to many areas of your business. Take some time to review the marketing and sales plan for post-launch activities. Also, take a look at the goals and objectives you have set up to promote the launch of your new brand. Next, analyze which of these tactics should continue into the post-launch activities as well as into your overall marketing and sales strategy.

Strong goals and objectives allow you to have measurable tactics.

9.2 Post-Launch Marketing and Sales

We spent time in the marketing and sales section talking about how vital the strategy is for the launch of your new brand. This is a great time to review that document with your team. You might remember the old adage that it takes up to seven touchpoints to get a potential customer to consider your product or service. With today's technology and social media, that number has more than doubled as people are inundated with hundreds of messages every hour.

At post-launch, it is also a great time to sit down with your marketing and sales teams to review the brand story. In addition to your hot topics, ask everyone the following questions. Do you have any feedback? Are there any changes we should make to our brand story? Are there any adjustments to be made before we make the next big push?

Although you tackled many of these items earlier in the initial launch, you should conduct a thorough review and make any necessary changes moving forward.

9.3 Brand Champions

Brand Champions are important for sales. In addition to your employees, friends, and family, your new customers are also Brand Champions! They will help spread the awesomeness of your brand and connect people they already know to your business.

Below are a few ideas we have successfully used with our clients to help them evolve their brands with Brand Champions. Think about how you might implement these ideas with your brand.

- **Case Studies:** During the launch, look for opportunities to generate content that can be used for case studies in your post-launch strategy.
- **Video Interviews:** Videos are very popular. You can shoot videos during the initial launch and showcase them post-launch.
- **Start a Blog:** Start this process early so you can build deep amounts of content. Do you have any Brand Champions that are willing to write a blog about how cool your brand is?
- As mentioned before, **Social Media** is here to stay. Have a plan and keep your social media up to date. Engage, engage, engage. Social media is a conversation that engages your customers.

- **Testimonials:** People prefer to buy brands from people they trust. Get these as often as possible.

9.4 Review Brand Message and Story

There are ways to stay on brand message and continue to perfect your brand story. Gather your team at regular intervals to discuss significant topics that specifically affect your brand. Within your team, provide a schedule. Start out meeting on a bi-weekly basis and adjust the timing accordingly. In each meeting, review all aspects of the brand with the team and create an actionable list of to-dos. Areas to cover with your team are brand elements such as: brand message, value proposition, competitors, trends, and visual language. Add anything else you deem important at this time. Finally, review past and current feedback from customers about your new product or service and identify anything that can affect the overall brand perception.

Final Thoughts

Every brand has a story. Every brand has a unique offering. Every brand can be positioned for growth.

Building a brand takes time and patience. Even though there is a great amount of work that goes into building a brand, don't let the small details derail you from following your dream.

I have learned a lot in the past three decades, and it has been my pleasure sharing it with you. I hope you have enjoyed reading this book and have learned many helpful strategies and tactics to build a successful brand.

Brand Terminology

Brand - To put this simply, it is what a person feels and thinks when they hear your brand name. It is a combination of the factual and emotional connections one has with your brand.

Brand Ambassadors - Fully engaged employees or celebrities who are paid to help promote your brand.

Brand Awareness - The company's ability to get their brand in front of their buyer and the buyer's ability to recollect the company brand.

Brand Building - The process of defining the brand elements and enhancing brand equity.

Brand Champions - People that help promote your brand such as customers, family, friends, and employees.

Brand Character - Similar to a person's demeanor. A brand can also embrace and communicate these characteristics (calm, smart, friendly, etc.).

Make My Brand Bigger

Brand Culture - The brand culture is directly related to the company culture and how employees live, work, play, and solve problems. It is very similar to the company culture.

Brand Elements - A specific identification of all brand elements necessary to build a successful brand such as brand position, brand differentiators, brand tone, brand character, brand awareness, and brand essence.

Brand Essence - A company's brand essence serves as the nucleus or center of every communication point. Therefore, all communications to the consumer are as clear and uniform as possible. The brand essence is the primary keyword that consumers associate with a company, service, or product.

Brand Equity - A brand's net worth.

Brand Experience - The feeling an individual has with a brand's actions. Their response to the brand's product or service, communications, marketing, design, identity, etc.

Brand Identity - The tangible and visual elements of the brand. Brand identity can include colors, design, logotype, etc. It is what appeals to your audience's senses. This is the overall look and something you can see, touch, feel, smell, and watch.

Brand Initiative - The successful development of the brand through identification of the brand's identity, marketing strategy, and competitive position.

Brand Loyalty - Your customers love your brand and are dedicated regardless of your competitor's actions.

Brand Message - The core message used for every communication with your buyer that influences and motivates them to act. The brand message integrates the value proposition.

Brand Personality - A set of human characteristics associated with a brand. How the brand behaves. Brand personality is both distinctive and enduring, and it is the outcome of the consumer's experience with the brand.

Brand Promise - Sets the brand expectations for the buyer. The perceived value proposition your buyer has about your brand.

Brand Positioning - How the brand is positioned against its competitors.

Brand Purpose - The purpose of your brand and how it servers your customers. The brand's purpose is directly connected to the needs of the consumer and should be straightforward, unique and specific. The pinnacle of how one might decide if the product or service offering is right for them or not.

Brand Standards Guide - A document that sets guidelines and rules of how the brand will be expressed throughout all communications.

Brand Story - The narrative in which you communicate your brand.

Make My Brand Bigger

Brand Strategy - This is the roadmap for the brand. Brand Strategy builds upon the vision of the brand. It defines the brand differentiation, value proposition and positioning. Brand strategy must align with all stakeholders: internal, external and the media.

Brand Tone - The tone is how the brand is communicated and how it is directly aligned with your brand character and personality.

Brand Value - The amount of money people are willing to pay for your product or service.

Brand Vision - Short and long-term vision of the brand's direction from the perspective of the owner or senior leaders.

Customer Experience - The interaction between your customer and your brand.

Discovery Process - The review of critical business and brand elements used to rebrand or build a new brand.

Differentiators - Determines what brand qualities separate your brand from your competitor's brand.

Positioning - A direct correlation between the perception of your brand and your competitors.

Rebranding - A branding and communications strategy used to take an existing brand and either refine or develop a new position in the marketplace.

Rebrand Initiative - The successful refinement of the brand through identification of the brand's identity, marketing strategy and competitive position.

Secret Sauce - The company or brand's unique and secret recipe which provides a competitive advantage.

SWOT Analysis - A process of defining your brand's strengths, weaknesses, opportunities, and threats.

Trademark Name - A trademarked word or name used to identify a brand.

Touchpoints - Every single interaction people have with your brand.

Value Proposition - Makes it clear to the buyer the primary reason why they are buying the product or service.

Visual Brand Audit - An analysis of all printed and digital brand communication pieces.

About the Author

Alex Valderrama is one of the nation's top brand strategists, award-winning designer, author, and the principal at Cranium Agency. Through his unique experience working with hundreds of clients, he has helped many brands lead in their industry with business growth, brand strategy and customer experience design.

Alex has worked with some of most well-known brands such as Truven Health Analytics, IBM, Principal Financial, Maytag Corporation, Citi Community Capital, Microsoft, Massey Ferguson, Wells Fargo, Gates Rubber Company, National CineMedia, Fathom Events, and many others.

At the International Academy of Design, Alex earned his BFA with an emphasis in Visual Communications. He also achieved the honor of summa cum laude. Alex has taught advanced branding and marketing courses at Arapahoe Community College and Metropolitan State University in Denver, Colorado, and he has been the curriculum advisor to several universities as well as a mentor to both students and interns.

Alex has served as a judge for several national branding and marketing competitions. He regularly lectures on branding and marketing throughout the design community and the business sector. Alex has also served as a marketing board member and independent branding advisor for several community development projects, non-profit organizations, business groups, and marketing associations. Additionally, Alex has held several board positions with the local American Institute of Graphic Arts (AIGA) and Business Marketing Association (BMA) chapters.

Cranium Agency, of which Alex is the founder, has received over 80 national and international awards from esteemed industry competitions such as Print Magazine, Graphis, and American Corporate Identity. Alex frequently writes about branding, and his design work has appeared in over 20 international publications such as The Big Book of Logos 3, The Best of Business Card Design 5, Blue is Hot, Red is Cool, Direct Response Graphics Book, Rockport's Letterhead, Logo Design 6 Source Book, and Best of Brochure Design 5 just to name a few.

Alex lives in Denver with his wife, Laurie, and enjoys reading, writing, drawing, hiking fourteeners, trail running, and spending as much time as possible with his grandkids Valon and Kennedy.